D0035724

Comments on other *Amazing Stories* from readers & reviewers

"*Tightly written volumes filled with lots of wit and humour about famous and infamous Canadians.*"
Eric Shackleton, *The Globe and Mail*

"*The heightened sense of drama and intrigue, combined with a good dose of human interest is what sets* Amazing Stories *apart.*"
Pamela Klaffke, *Calgary Herald*

"*This is popular history as it should be... For this price, buy two and give one to a friend.*"
Terry Cook, a reader from Ottawa, on **Rebel Women**

"*Glasner creates the moment of the explosion itself in graphic detail...she builds detail upon gruesome detail to create a convincingly authentic picture.*"
Peggy McKinnon, *The Sunday Herald*, on **The Halifax Explosion**

"*It was wonderful...I found I could not put it down. I was sorry when it was completed.*"
Dorothy F. from Manitoba on **Marie-Anne Lagimodière**

"*Stories are rich in description, and bristle with a clever, stylish realness.*"
Mark Weber, *Central Alberta Advisor*, on **Ghost Town Stories II**

"*A compelling read. Bertin...has selected only the most intriguing tales, which she narrates with a wealth of detail.*"
Joyce Glasner, *New Brunswick Reader*, on **Strange Events**

"*The resulting book is one readers will want to share with all the women in their lives.*"
Lynn Martel, *Rocky Mountain Outlook*, on **Women Explorers**

LEGENDS, LIARS, AND LAWBREAKERS

AMAZING STORIES

LEGENDS, LIARS, AND LAWBREAKERS

Incredible Tales from the Pacific Northwest

HISTORY/CRIME

by Valerie Green

PUBLISHED BY ALTITUDE PUBLISHING CANADA LTD.
1500 Railway Avenue, Canmore, Alberta T1W 1P6
www.altitudepublishing.com
1-800-957-6888

Copyright 2004 © Valerie Green
All rights reserved
First published 2004

Extreme care has been taken to ensure that all information presented in
this book is accurate and up to date. Neither the author nor the
publisher can be held responsible for any errors.

Publisher	Stephen Hutchings
Associate Publisher	Kara Turner
Series Editor	Jill Foran
Digital Photo Coloration	Scott Manktelow

We acknowledge the financial support of the Government
of Canada through the Book Publishing Industry Development
Program (BPIDP) for our publishing activities.

Altitude GreenTree Program 🌲
Altitude Publishing will plant twice as many trees as were used
in the manufacturing of this product.

National Library of Canada Cataloguing in Publication Data

Green, Valerie, 1940-
Legends, liars, and lawbreakers / Valerie Green.

(Amazing stories)
Includes bibliographical references.
ISBN 1-55153-771-0

1. Criminals--British Columbia--Biography. 2. Criminals--Washington (State)--
Biography. 3. Impostors and imposture--British Columbia--Biography. 4.
Impostors and imposture--Washington (State)--Biography. 5. British Columbia
--Biography. 6. Washington (State)--Biography. I. Title. II. Series:
Amazing stories (Canmore, Alta.)

FC3805.G74 2004   971.1'0099   C2004-901178-2

An application for the trademark for Amazing Stories™
has been made and the registered trademark is pending.

Printed and bound in Canada by Friesens
2 4 6 8 9 7 5 3 1

Cover: Mug shots of James Mahoney, Henry Ferguson, Mary Smith, and Bill Byrd
(Courtesy of the Washington State Archives)

To my Seattle friends, Terese, Julio, and Juanita,
for their encouragement and endless inspiration.

Contents

Prologue

He was exhausted — beyond exhausted, actually. Every muscle in his body ached, and the pain shooting up his leg told him that the bullet had done far more damage than he'd first imagined. The sun was beating down on him, and though his vision was blurred, he knew without having to look down that he was losing a great deal of blood at a very rapid rate.

The random shots he'd fired back at his pursuers had all been way off target because of that cursed sun in his eyes. His leg throbbing, he realized he would have to crawl to safety, so he began to drag his weakened body along the ground.

He paused for a moment in the field, hidden by the tall wheat that seemed to whisper in the warm breeze. Perhaps if he attempted to make a tourniquet around his leg it would stop the blood. Perhaps. But was it worth it? The agony was now more than he could bear. But still he refused to let them take him alive. He had vowed long ago never to let that happen.

With only one bullet left, the decision was remarkably easy to make. That bullet was meant for one person, and one person only.

He raised the gun slowly, and fired.

Chapter 1
The Nisqually Chief Who Forgave His Enemies

n February 19, 1858, Leschi, chief of the Nisqually, mounted the steps to the gallows with his head held high. Military guards flanked him, and the Reverend Louis Rossi, a French Catholic missionary, walked by his side.

After almost three years of imprisonment, Leschi was weak and emaciated, but as he gazed at the crowd of onlookers, he caught sight of Antonio Rabbeson and was overcome by a sudden burst of strength. Rabbeson had been the principal witness against him at his trial. Leschi called out to the man in anger, denouncing him as a liar who had never once been able to tell the truth.

Reverend Rossi, who just a few days earlier had converted the Nisqually chief to Christianity, was disappointed by this angry outburst. However, Leschi's anger disappeared as quickly as it came, and the chief was calm again as his hands and legs were bound and the noose was placed around his neck. Seeming to accept his fate, he looked out at the now silent crowd and addressed it for the last time, saying, "I forgive them all."

* * *

Chief Leschi was born in 1808 in a small village at the tip of the Puget Sound. His father, Sennatco, was portage chief of the Nisqually, and his mother was the daughter of a Yakima chief. Legend has it that on the day Leschi was born, a star rose over the Nisqually Plains, proclaiming him as leader of his people.

Leschi grew to medium height, and his appearance bore many Yakima features — his broad shoulders, aquiline nose, firm jaw, and sloping forehead were all telling signs of his maternal ancestry. An intelligent, peace-loving young man, Leschi possessed powerful oratory skills and was often called upon to settle disputes within his own tribe. These disputes, however, were few and far between. For the most part, the

Nisqually led peaceful lives, sharing their hunting grounds along the Nisqually River with other tribes in the region. Situated in the northern portion of Washington State, the Nisqually River flows 78 miles from its source at the glacier on Mount Rainier to its delta in the Puget Sound, traversing a land of towering firs and abundant wildlife. The existence of the Nisqually people was initially governed by the unwritten laws of that land; any problems or disputes that did arise were usually minor.

Things began to change when the Americans and the British laid claim to land in nearby Oregon County. In 1824, the fur-trading Hudson's Bay Company (HBC) built Fort Vancouver on the banks of the Columbia River, and in 1833, Fort Nisqually was built on the Puget Sound. Soon after that, the Nisqually Plains were also claimed by the HBC, and renamed the Puget Sound Agricultural Farmland.

Leschi then decided to watch things more closely. The British, many of whom had come without wives, began to take Nisqually women in marriage. At first, Leschi was satisfied with this arrangement; a good relationship had developed between the two cultures, and his people were always treated well. He and his brother, Quiemuth, even accepted positions with the HBC as horse tenders.

Chief Leschi

Things took a turn for the worse in 1846, when the international boundary was set at the 49th parallel. Many more Americans (known then as "Bostons," which was a general term given to all white American settlers, some of whom had in fact come from Boston) began to infiltrate the Pacific Northwest and claim traditional tribal lands as their own. These people brought their families with them and started to build homes, thereby introducing the idea of "ownership of land," a concept that was totally foreign to the Nisqually. A United States Army fort was even established at Steilacoom, which is situated west of the Cascade Mountains near Lakewood. (Today, the restored fort is located near the entrance to the Western State Hospital.)

By March of 1853, Washington Territory was officially established, and Isaac Stevens was appointed governor and superintendent of Indian Affairs. Western Washington was then divided into treaty districts, and Leschi was one of the five Native chiefs appointed over a district. That same year, Governor Stevens drafted the Medicine Creek Treaty, which offered the Nisqually peoples schools, hunting and fishing rights, blacksmith shops, and land to live on. But while it appeared the Nisqually were being offered many benefits, the reality was that the government would have sole authority over the tribe and where its people could live.

In December of 1854, the Medicine Creek Treaty was formally presented to the leaders of the Nisqually and neighboring tribes, all of who were asked to sign. Leschi could immediately see that many of the requests he had put forward, such as rights to specific portions of the river for fishing, and prairie land for the tribes' horses, were not being addressed in the treaty. There was also an unwritten threat that the tribes might later be moved to the more northern territories. In effect, Leschi saw the Medicine Creek Treaty as utterly unjust, and he refused to sign it. (Oddly enough, an "X" still appeared on the treaty beside his name.)

The Nisqually people stood firm behind Leschi's decision not to sign, and hostilities grew. Nonetheless, Governor Stevens continued to pursue the signing of other treaties with tribes in northern and eastern Washington. While he was off doing that, Leschi decided to go to the new capital, Olympia, to meet with the acting governor, Charles Mason. There he promised to uphold the peace if his people were allowed to stay on their homeland and retain their fishing rights. Unfortunately, his request was denied, and no agreement was reached. Leschi returned to his home feeling frustrated and depressed.

Tensions between the government and the Nisqually continued to mount. In order to prevent an uprising, Acting Governor Mason ordered the arrest of Leschi and his brother. He wanted them brought back to Olympia, more for their own protection than anything else. By that time, however, both Leschi and Quiemuth had taken their families and fled far into the northeast foothills, where other members of their tribe soon joined them. Leschi was chosen as their leader and given the title of War Chief of the Allied Indian Forces.

Meanwhile, a detachment of volunteers, formed by the governor, followed the Nisqually into the hills in the hopes of apprehending Leschi and Quiemuth. During a skirmish with a band of roving warriors at Connell's Prairie, two of the volunteers, Moses and Miles, were killed.

The Treaty War officially began in the fall of 1855. At all times, Leschi stressed to his warriors that the war was to be fought only against the government troops and not the area's settlers. However, on January 25, 1856, several settlers joined in the fighting when they began firing at a group of attacking Natives, who were also being bombarded by cannon fire from the navy sloop *Decatur*, anchored in Elliott Bay. This skirmish, which became known as the Battle of Seattle, was short-lived, but an estimated 100 Native people and two settlers — Milton Holgate and Robert Wilson — were killed. (The Battle of Seattle took its name from Chief Noah Sealth, after whom the city of Seattle was named. Ironically, during the course of the Treaty War, Chief Seattle stayed away from the action and took no part in the battles.)

Governor Stevens, by now very angry, demanded that the men responsible for the deaths of the settlers be brought to trial. He even named whom he believed were the five ringleaders, and Leschi was among them.

Doubtless Leschi had played a part in the Battle of Seattle, but he was also suspected, and later accused, of leading the ambush at Connell's Prairie back in 1855 — the ambush that had resulted in the deaths of two civilian volunteers. The governor was now determined to bring Leschi in to face trial, for this was a time in history when a white man who killed a Native received only minimum punishment, but a Native who killed a white man was punished with death.

As the search for the Nisqually chief intensified, rebel warrior groups continued to attack and kill civilian families along the White River. Soldiers and volunteer groups, however, soon outnumbered these warriors and put an end to the attacks.

Leschi, meanwhile, was still attempting to make peace. Early in 1856, he arranged for a private meeting with one of the few Bostons he trusted — an Indian agent named John Swan — in order to seek a renegotiation of the treaty. At that meeting, he learned that Governor Stevens refused to talk with him until "every savage who murdered the families on the White River [was] hanged by the neck." Although Leschi insisted that he had played no part in those attacks, the governor believed that he had, and claimed the chief was a liar.

In April of 1856, a group of Nisqually was completely annihilated while fishing the Nisqually River — a volunteer militia had attacked them under orders from Governor Stevens. The federal government then decided to intervene by advising Stevens to meet with the Medicine Creek Treaty Native tribes again and change the terms concerning the Nisqually and Puyallup reservations. Under the new terms, treaty lands would include Leschi's own village grounds at Muck Creek, and territory on both sides of the Nisqually River.

The Treaty War came to an end once the new terms were established, but there was still a price on the heads of Leschi and his brother. Quiemuth decided to give himself up to the governor and face the consequences. While he was being taken to Fort Steilacoom, he and his jailers stopped at Olympia for the night. As Quiemuth slept on the floor in the governor's office, someone entered the room and stabbed him to death. This unknown person was never captured or brought to trial.

Still a fugitive, Leschi continued to seek peace, even vowing to cut off his own hand to prove he would honor the terms of the treaty and never fight again. His words went unheeded. Then, in early November of 1856, his nephew Sluggia — a young man Leschi had raised as his own — betrayed him by giving information regarding his whereabouts to the authorities. Sluggia's reward for this betrayal was 50 blankets. He was later murdered by Leschi's friend, Wa-he-lut (Yelm Jim), in order to avenge the chief. Although Yelm Jim was arrested for this crime, he was pardoned on his execution day in 1860.

In mid-November of 1856, Leschi was finally captured and taken into the custody of Colonel Casey as a prisoner of war. Governor Stevens, however, also considered him a civilian criminal and formally charged him with the murder of two soldiers: Colonel A. Benton Moses and another man named Miles, both of whom were killed during the White River Ambush.

Over the next two years of his imprisonment, Leschi went to trial twice. At his first trial, the jury stood ten to two for conviction and a final verdict could not be reached. At his second trial, Leschi's attorneys, Frank Clark and H.O. Crosby (great-grandfather of singer Bing Crosby), introduced several key defense witnesses. The lawyers assumed that having such esteemed men as Chief Factor William Tolmie of the Hudson's Bay Company, Lieutenant August Kautz (the first man to lead a party up Mount Rainier), and well-known Pacific Northwest pioneer Ezra Meeker to speak on Leschi's behalf would work in his favor. But despite the words and support of these sterling men, Leschi was convicted.

The conviction was due mainly to the testimony of Antonio B. Rabbeson, a friend of Governor Stevens's, who swore on oath that he had witnessed Leschi and two other Natives fire the fatal shots at Moses and Miles. Leschi's lawyers argued that Leschi had not been the one to kill Colonel Moses, and that in any event, these men had been killed during warfare; both sides had experienced casualties and therefore an accused killer could not be tried in a civilian court.

After being found guilty, Leschi spoke through an interpreter, saying: "I do not know anything about your laws. I had supposed that the killing of armed men in wartime was not murder; if it was, the soldiers who killed Indians are guilty of murder too. I went to war because I believed that the Indian had been wronged by the white men, and I did everything in my power to beat the Boston soldiers, but, for lack of numbers, supplies and ammunition, I have failed. I deny that I had any part in the killing…As God sees me, this is the truth."

Leschi was first sentenced to hang on June 10, 1857, but this date was appealed. The appeal was unsuccessful, and his execution date was reset for January 22, 1858. Further delaying tactics by Leschi's supporters caused a third and final date to be set for February 19, 1858. Ironically, Ezra Meeker, who had voted to acquit Leschi at his trial, refused to try to stop the execution, and later admitted that he thought Leschi was "a patriotic martyr to Governor Isaac Stevens' political ambitions and ill-conceived policies."

Because it was deemed inappropriate for Leschi to be hanged on the grounds of a United States Army Fort, a scaffold was erected a mile to the east of Fort Steilacoom. On the morning of February 19, Leschi was taken from the guardroom at the fort, where he had been chained hand and foot in a small, open cell. For much of his imprisonment, he had been on view to onlookers who had witnessed his humiliation. But even after almost three years of confinement, he was still able to walk to the gallows with the pride of a great chief.

A few of his people, his wife among them, were there to witness the execution, and the soft beating of drums could be heard in the distance. As Leschi addressed the crowd with his final words of forgiveness, an eerie silence fell. Then, lowering his head, he prepared to meet his end. Hangman Charles Grainger later recalled: "He did not seem to be the least bit excited at all — nothing of the kind, and that is more than I could say for myself. In fact, Leschi seemed to be the coolest of any on the scaffold. He was in good flesh and had a firm step and mounted the scaffold without assistance, and as well as I did myself. I felt then I was hanging an innocent man, and I believe it yet."

After the execution, Leschi's body was released to the Nisqually peoples, and he was buried on tribal land. In 1895, his remains were moved to the mouth of Muck

Creek, close to where he had been hanged. He rested there until 1917, at which time that land became part of the Fort Lewis Military Reservation.

Today, Chief Leschi lies at peace in the Cushman Indian Cemetery in Tacoma, Washington, on the grounds of the Puyallup Indian Reservation. On the back of his headstone are the words: "Chief Leschi, 1808–1858. Judicially murdered on February 19, 1858, owing to a misunderstanding of the Treaty of 1854–1855. Serving his people by his death. Sacrificed to a principle. A martyr to liberty, honor and the rights of his native land. Erected by those he died to serve."

In the fall of 1996, the Chief Leschi School, a school operated by the Puyallup Tribe and situated in the shadow of Mount Rainier, was officially opened to serve Native American students from 92 different tribes. Current enrollment is over 800 students — a fitting memorial to a great chief.

Chapter 2
The Flying Dutchman

enry Ferguson was a tough, bold, and extremely dangerous felon. At the turn of the 20th century, Western Washington was plagued by a variety of scoundrels and thieves, but Ferguson's audacious adventures as a smuggler set him apart from these other criminals.

It was a time in Washington State's history when the laws of the land were easy to circumvent if a person possessed a little ingenuity or a whole lot of daring. Ferguson had both. For years he operated in the San Juans, a group of islands which separate Canada from the United States. Somewhat mystical in character, the San Juan Islands have been shaped by centuries of

Prisoner 2633, Henry Ferguson

weathering and the passing of several ice ages. Their incredible beauty has been carved out through time and, because they boast a milder climate than the rest of Western Washington (which is known for its wet weather), they are often referred to as the "banana belt."

In addition, it seems that the particular geographical location of the islands also separated them from the rules and regulations that governed most other places. When the international border between Canada and the

United States was set in 1846 at the 49th parallel, it appeared as though the San Juan Islands had been completely overlooked — at least when it came to the laws of the land. An ongoing battle as to who actually owned the islands — Canada or the U.S. — continued until 1872, when a mediator awarded them to the U.S. and placed the international boundary at the Haro Strait.

This decision still allowed for a small area in the Haro Strait, roughly four miles from the Canadian shoreline and two miles from the San Juan Islands, to serve as a sort of no man's land. The area was easily accessible, and soon became inundated by smugglers whose vessels plied the waterways between the two countries with their illegal contraband. With the borderline between the two countries taking a somewhat circuitous route through the islands, it was difficult for the authorities to keep track of all the illegal activities taking place. Consequently, it seemed that smuggling had been going on there since time immemorial.

The people of the islands tolerated the smuggling that took place around their homes because, for the most part, they felt they had nothing to fear from the smugglers. The one exception was Henry Ferguson, who quickly became the meanest and toughest smuggler of them all, terrifying not only the island people, but also settlers from Vancouver Island to Olympia.

According to police historian Cecil Clark, the first contraband to cross the Haro Strait was back in the 1860s, when barrels of whiskey were peddled to American troops stationed on the San Juan Islands. Once this particular scheme was uncovered, the bootleggers involved were placed in the military guardroom there, and their stock was repossessed.

Later, when the San Juans were officially United States territory, they became an ideal place to store the opium being smuggled throughout the Puget Sound. This raw opium came directly from China and was processed in Victoria, British Columbia, in five licensed factories. At that time, there was no Canadian law against possession of opium in any amount.

Smuggling then continued in the form of human cargo. Illegal aliens (mostly Chinese) were loaded into small boats at Victoria's inner harbor, or at Maynard's Cove (known today as Smugglers' Cove at Ten Mile Point) on Vancouver Island, and taken across the border to the United States under cover of night. This type of smuggling continued well into the 1890s, at which time Henry Ferguson arrived on the scene.

Ferguson came to the Pacific Northwest from Wyoming, where he had spent time as a member of Butch Cassidy's Hole In The Wall Gang. Reportedly the last surviving member of that notorious gang, Ferguson had already developed his villainous reputation long before he arrived in Washington State. It was known throughout the United States that he thought nothing of robbing and killing to survive. Like other members of the Hole in the Wall Gang, he had robbed countless banks and trains, and anyone who got in his way usually ended up dead.

Ferguson made the decision to head north when his encounters with vigilantes and U.S. cavalrymen were becoming far too frequent for comfort in Wyoming. Indeed, he had felt it advisable to leave while he still could. During his travels west, he changed his name to Henry Wagner, but he by no means changed his unlawful ways. The life of the outlaw was in his blood. Upon arrival in the San Juans, he was soon upholding his reputation as an audacious outlaw of the first degree.

A later Wanted Poster described Ferguson as five feet ten inches tall, with dark hair and steel-gray eyes that were said to penetrate and terrify. He never traveled without his .44 caliber Colt revolver or his double-barreled shotgun, and he always wore a black cap when aboard his boat, and a light-colored canvas hat whenever he was ashore.

Ferguson's exploits in the San Juans were reported to be so daring and swift that no one knew exactly where

BURGLARY

Wanted for Postoffice, Store and Launch Burglary.

The Postoffice at Langley, on Whidby Island, Wash., across from Everett, was robbed on the night of July 15, 1909, and the safe looted of $176.80. Admission was gained with skeleton key and combination of the safe worked or had not been locked.

The burglary was committed by Henry Ferguson, John McDonald and Nels J. Jorgenson. McDonald and Jorgensen were captured. Ferguson is still at large.

Water Pirate Henry Ferguson; alias "Jack the Flying Dutchman" whose description is as follows: Age 39; heighth 5 feet 10 inches; hair dark and may be a little gray; eyes steel gray; medium complexion; weiggt about 180 pounds; a little bow legged, and is a little stooped. Water pirate; wears black cap when in boat and light-colored canvass hat when on shore. Is generally armed with a 44-calibre Colt's revolver and carries it in his right hip pocket, and a double-barreled shot-gun with 17-inch barrels. He has a 16-ft. long, square and copper painted boat with small deck forward and apt, 3 horse power gasoline engine, Phirro make, small sail, no cabin when last seen, but may have repainted the boat. Ferguson is probably accompanied by a man by the name of Wm Juhan, described as follows: height about 5 ft. 5½ in. dark hair; eyes brown; complexion dark; about 36 years old, and a half-breed Indian woman, all of whom are supposed to be in Nanaimo, B. C., or vicinity, as their plan was to rob a company store at that place. Both of these men are desperate characters, and I am informed left here about a week ago for B. C. for the purpose of murdering two men and committing a robbery.

Ferguson is well posted on the B. C. waters and on Puget Sound. He talks about Yulu Island, Frazer river and Bring Berge Island.

Ferguson is an ex-convict and is wanted in Island county for burglary, and his capture is of the utmost importance on account of the crimes he has committed and for those he threatens to commit.

I am very anxious to get this man and will appreciate any information which may lead to his arrest.

Wire any information at my expense.

MARKUS WANGSNESS,
Sheriff of Island County.
Coupeville, Washington.

or when he would strike next. Before embarking on a new smuggling escapade, he would steal a boat to use for the job. Then, when the job was completed and he had delivered the goods, he would immediately paint the boat a different color so that it became unrecognizable to authorities. Ferguson always operated this way, and because he moved so swiftly from one crime to the next, he was soon nicknamed "The Flying Dutchman." His crimes included smuggling opium and human cargo, and stealing from log booms and fish traps.

Of course, Ferguson didn't stop there. Brandishing his guns, he also began looting warehouses and commandeering cargoes from the small Puget Sound freighters. He was the typical pirate: nothing was beyond his scope, and nothing was sacred.

Ferguson continued to move around the islands speedily, eluding authorities at every turn and using a number of hideouts along the way. He lived on the lam, seeking shelter where he could and hiding his money in various places. Among his several hideaways was an isolated cabin on Skagit Island. This island was also the domain of Benjamin Ure, who had made it his business to shelter criminals like Ferguson. Ure had once been a wealthy landowner, but had lost most of his real estate over time. He had also worked in the customs service, and therefore knew all the ins and outs of bypassing the law. After having enjoyed his own stint as a rum smuggler, Ure took pleasure in harboring others of a similar persuasion on his island.

However, it was while hiding out on Skagit Island in October of 1901 that Ferguson was cornered in the cabin, and then captured after a prolonged shootout with sheriff's officers. It is not known whether someone had squealed on Ferguson, but because he had many enemies, it is more than likely that one of them had reported his whereabouts to the authorities.

On December 7, 1901, Ferguson was charged in the Snohomish County Court in Everett with warehouse robbery. He was sentenced to 14 years in the Washington State Penitentiary at Walla Walla, with hard labor.

Amazingly enough, in 1908, a mere seven years into his sentence, the Parole Board decided to release Ferguson back into society. Prison officials recommended "final discharge for faithful services rendered the institution and for exemplary conduct." The notorious pirate had proved he could behave himself behind bars.

But it was all an incredible ploy, and authorities had made an enormous mistake by releasing him. Ferguson had acted the part of the reformed criminal with conviction, but almost immediately after his release, he returned to his old lawless lifestyle. His time in prison had by no means changed him.

On the night of July 15, 1909, the Flying Dutchman, in company with John McDonald and Nels J. Jorgensen, robbed the post office at Langley on Whidbey Island, looting the safe of $176.80. Both McDonald and Jorgensen were captured, but a Wanted Poster was put out for Ferguson, who remained at large.

Ferguson was indicted by a grand jury *in absentia*, and Prosecuting Attorney Elmer Todd made arrangements for the financing of a wide search for this reprehensible criminal, who was still successfully managing to elude the law. For three years the search continued, until funds ran out and it was deemed a failure.

The decision by the federal government back in 1908 to finally come down on the lucrative 50-year-old opium trade had merely encouraged men like Ferguson to continue smuggling it, just as prohibition later created a whole new era of rum-running across the Haro Strait. In Ferguson's case, the decision had also made him broaden his crimes to the robbing of post offices, which soon proved highly profitable for him. In 1912, Ferguson boldly robbed the very same Langley post office he had hit in 1909, stealing not only government cash, but also the safe that contained it.

By this time, he was traveling with an accomplice named William Julian (or Juhan), and an unknown

Native woman. When the Wanted Poster for Ferguson's capture was put up by the sheriff of Island County in Coupeville, Washington, the threesome were thought to be heading for Nanaimo, on Vancouver Island. The fugitives were considered to be "desperate characters," for it was said that they had threatened to murder two men on Vancouver Island, and to commit another robbery there.

Early in March of 1913, two constables at Union Bay, near Nanaimo, were staking out a store in the hopes of catching a burglar who had already broken into the establishment twice before. Around midnight, they noticed a light inside the store and went to investigate with their own flashlight. Upon entering, they spotted two suspects, one of whom was pointing a .44 caliber revolver straight at them. Constable Ross immediately turned off his light and yelled a warning to his partner, Westaway, but it was too late. A shot was fired; the bullet grazed Constable Ross's shoulder and then struck Westaway in the chest.

Ross managed to lunge at the shooter and, after a brief struggle, was able to handcuff and arrest him. The man was identified from the Wanted Poster as Harry Ferguson, and was taken into custody to be tried for the murder of Constable Harry Westaway, as well as wounding a sheriff and killing a postmaster in Washington

State. He was sentenced in a Canadian court to death by hanging.

Back in prison again, Ferguson tried to end his own life by beating his head against a brick wall, vowing he would never allow himself to be hanged for his crimes. His suicide attempt was unsuccessful and, on August 28, 1913, after calmly drinking his last cup of coffee, he walked to the scaffold in Nanaimo and finally met a destiny that had long since been mapped out for him.

A rather macabre aside to Ferguson's hanging was the fact that his hangman, Arthur Ellus, was especially pleased to be executing the infamous killer on that particular morning. With Ferguson's death, Ellis became the record-holder for the most hangings carried out in Canada. Up until that day, the record had been held by his uncle.

Chapter 3
The Man Who Terrorized a State

t was August 1902, and Harry Tracy had been running from the law for far too long. He was gaunt, underfed, and exhausted. Most men in his condition would have given up by then, but Tracy was different. He refused to accept defeat. After having traveled over 400 miles across Washington State with a large bounty on his head, and leaving behind a trail of dead bodies as he outwitted his pursuers at every turn, he was more determined than ever to avoid capture. His will to survive was paramount.

As he traveled down a dusty road outside Creston in Lincoln County, Tracy met a young man by the name

of George Goldfinch and decided to take him hostage —
a habit he'd developed while running from the law.
Needing to build up his waning strength, Tracy planned
to hold Goldfinch hostage while he rested and ate at a
nearby farmhouse belonging to the Eddy family.

But by this time, Tracy's luck was running out.
While he was making himself comfortable at the Eddy
ranch, two sheriffs who were following up on an informant's tip were forming a posse and preparing to
descend on the criminal. On the evening of August 5,
the sheriffs arrived at the ranch and quickly spotted
Tracy leaving the barn. He had left his rifle inside the
building, and only carried a revolver.

The officers, realizing they had finally cornered the
most cold-blooded killer in Washington State history,
ordered Tracy to raise his hands.

* * *

Harry Tracy was born in 1874 in Poughkeepsie, New
York, a quiet river town in the Hudson Valley. As a young
boy he was restless and always seemed to get into trouble. By the time he was a teenager, he had developed an
attitude of complete disdain for the law, and was hell-
bent on destruction. He soon left home and headed for
the city of Boston, where he embraced a life of crime.

Before long, he was well known to the Boston police force, whose officers were reportedly so intimated by the young thug that most refused to arrest him without plenty of backup help. Even back then, Tracy was considered dangerous and evil. In order to escape the consequences of his many crimes, which included a vicious attack on a man and woman in a local brothel, Tracy eventually did Boston a favor and headed west.

By the mid 1890s, Tracy was serving time in a Utah prison for burglary. There, he met fellow convict Dave Lant, and in 1897, the two men made the first of many jailbreaks. Tracy and Lant then sought refuge in Brown's Hole — an isolated valley stretching through Colorado, Utah, and Wyoming — where they met up with Butch Cassidy's "Wild Bunch" gang.

Formed in 1896, the Wild Bunch was a notorious gang of outlaws that included such bandits as Harvey Logan, Harry Longabaugh, Ben Kilpatrick, Elzy Lay, and George Curry. Tracy was now consorting with the cream of the criminal crop. Most of these men thought nothing of killing in cold blood while robbing banks and trains.

On March 1, 1898, Harry Tracy, Dave Lant, and Patrick Louis "Swede" Johnson found themselves in a confrontation with the law. Johnson was a fellow criminal who, two weeks earlier, had killed a 15-year-old named Will Strang at the Red Creek Ranch simply because the boy hadn't moved quickly enough to get him a horse from the corral. Tracy and Lant had met up with Swede on the trail shortly after that killing.

The three men then fled back to Brown's Hole, but a posse, led by Red Creek Ranch owner Valentine Hoy, soon caught up to them. Hoy approached the dangerous trio on foot, and though Tracy warned him to stop, he continued to walk towards them. Hoy's bravery — or perhaps his stupidity — cost him his life; one of Tracy's bullets pierced the ranch owner's heart, and the rest of the posse temporarily retreated.

Later, the posse resumed its pursuit, and eventually caught and arrested Tracy. He was back in jail — but not for long. Out of a desperate need for survival and freedom, he had developed Houdini-like escape tactics. It seemed no bars could hold him once he devised a plan of escape. However, shortly after his second jailbreak, he was recaptured and once again placed in custody.

After yet another escape from confinement, Tracy fled to Oregon where, in 1899, he met an outlaw by the name of Dave Merrill at a gambling saloon in Portland. The two men looked very much alike, and many people mistook them for twins. Both had a way with the opposite sex, though women were especially drawn to Tracy's good looks and gentlemanly manner. Merrill's sister, Rose, was no exception. She and Tracy were married that same year and settled into a cottage near the Willamette River.

But even married life could not reform Tracy. He and his new brother-in-law were soon involved in a series of store and bank robberies throughout Oregon. They wore masks when conducting the robberies, and became known as the "False Face Bandits." The two men were eventually apprehended and sentenced to serve time in the Oregon State Penitentiary for their crimes — Tracy to 20 years and Merrill to 13.

Before long, Tracy decided once again that he'd had enough of prison life and set about making preparations for yet another escape. On the morning of June 9, 1902, these plans came to fruition. As the prisoners were marched out to the yard that morning to be counted by guards, Tracy fired a shot at one guard, who died instantly. Everyone in the yard was thrown into a state of shock by this sudden turn of events; prisoners were not expected to have rifles inside a prison! But Tracy was no ordinary prisoner. He had somehow managed to contact his criminal friends on the outside, and someone (possibly his wife) had smuggled two Winchesters into the prison yard.

Assisted by Merrill, Tracy began firing wildly at other guards. A prisoner who was serving a life sentence tried to disarm Tracy, but his good intentions cost him a bullet from the second rifle in the hands of Merrill.

After grabbing a nearby ladder, Tracy and Merrill climbed the prison wall and began firing more shots at the fence patrol guards, killing one and wounding two others. The escapees then picked up one of the wounded guards and used him as a shield as they headed off into the woods. There they killed him in cold blood, took his rifle, and disappeared from sight.

In total, three men had been killed during the course of the prison escape, and Harry Tracy and Dave Merrill were now considered extremely dangerous felons. They had to be captured at all costs. By late morning, the sheriff of nearby Salem, Oregon, had ordered every able-bodied man with a gun who lived within 50 miles of the prison to take part in the hunt.

The two criminals, however, were seasoned professionals when it came to outwitting the law. They managed to elude the authorities all that day, and by nightfall had passed through Salem on their way north. As they traveled, the convicts held up two men and forced them to hand over their clothes. Then, at the Felix Labaucher stables, they helped themselves to two fast horses.

The next day, the Washington State Penitentiary joined in the chase by sending down bloodhounds to follow the convicts' scent, but because Tracy and Merrill had new clothing and fast horses, the scent was soon lost. It appeared, however, that the pair was heading north to Washington State, and the audacity of their escapades over the next few days was nothing short of astounding. They already possessed a good arsenal of weaponry but, at one point, managed to challenge two men in a pursuing posse and relieve them of their weapons. Company F of the Oregon State National Guard and a group of over 100 men could not even stop the twosome.

The reward for their capture continued to increase; a bounty of $8000 hung over Tracy's head alone. However, after five days of searching, the resources and stamina of the exhausted posse were depleted. By then, Tracy had persuaded a farmer to row him and his partner across the Columbia River and into Washington State, where Sheriff Marsh of Clark County took up the chase with relish. Of course, the sheriff had no idea just how hopeless his task would be, or how much destruction Harry Tracy would cause in his state over the coming weeks. Though two men from Marsh's posse did manage to temporarily corner the convicts early on in the chase, Tracy and Merrill were once again able to escape capture, and for many days their trail appeared to be lost.

Then, early on the morning of July 2, a mysterious

looking vagrant was spotted in the Puget Sound area at an oyster fishery managed by Horatio Alling. The vagrant stood for a moment in the doorway of the office where Alling and two of his men were working, and then spoke. "I'm Tracy, the convict," he said. "I want something to eat right away. If you're quiet and don't raise a fuss, I won't harm you."

Noticing the gun in Tracy's hand, the men were not about to argue the point. They also agreed to summon the captain of a nearby launch, and listened while Tracy ordered the captain and his son to get up steam and take him into Seattle. The convict then helped himself to some clothes and, before leaving, tied up Alling and his men.

While riding the boat into Seattle, Tracy stayed at one end of the small cabin, his gun resting on his knee the whole time. For the next 12 hours he remained completely in control of the situation. His reputation for killing people at the slightest provocation was well known, and the captain and his crew had no intention of crossing him or disobeying his orders. Tracy even joked with the captain, but his body never relaxed its steadfast vigil, and his steel blue eyes were constantly on the lookout for trouble.

One of the men onboard eventually worked up the courage to ask Tracy where Merrill was. "I killed him!"

Tracy replied, not missing a beat. He called Merrill a no-good coward who was always ready to bolt. "He was frightened to death all the time. It made me angry when the newspapers gave him half the credit for our escape!" he added.

Tracy then told the captain and crew that he and Merrill had had a bitter argument after he'd called him a coward. The pair had decided to settle their dispute by means of a shootout but, according to Tracy, Merrill had haggled over the terms.

"I knew he meant to play false," said Tracy. "I couldn't trust him, so when I had taken eight steps forward, I fired over my shoulder and hit him in the back. That first shot didn't finish him off so I shot him again. He got what he deserved." Two weeks later, Merrill's body was found, with two bullets in it, near Chehalis in Lewis County, halfway between Portland and Seattle.

During the entire boat ride, which he later referred to as his "yachting trip," Tracy continued to display a complete disregard for human life. At one point he ordered the captain to run the boat close to a military prison on McNeil's Island so that he could take a pot shot at one of the guards.

At Meadow Point, near Seattle, Tracy tied up the captain and crew and, taking one man at gunpoint as his guide, went ashore. He then released his captive and headed, on foot, towards the north end of Lake Washington. Many people thought they recognized him on the road, but no one was completely sure. Eventually he reached the town of Bothell (12 miles northeast of Seattle), where he lay down in the dense bush to enjoy some much needed sleep.

Meanwhile, the entire Seattle area was on alert. Doors were bolted and guns were brought out. Numerous posses were formed. Sheriff Cudihee of King County took up the hunt next, vowing never to stop following Tracy's trail until the vicious criminal was brought to justice. Although other sheriffs had given up once Tracy had left their particular jurisdiction, Cudihee was different. For him, the capture of Harry Tracy became a personal vendetta, and he was determined to win.

Over the coming days, varying reports surfaced regarding Tracy's whereabouts. Posses were sent out in all directions to cover these reports. One group went to a brickyard after someone claimed to have spotted the convict there. Another posse set off along the railway tracks towards Pontiac. This group consisted of two officers from Everett, several from Seattle, and a reporter from the *Seattle Times*. Making their way along the tracks, the men spotted some cabins surrounded by old tree stumps and freshly beaten-down grass. They all agreed that this looked a likely place for Tracy to hide out.

And they were right. As the posse approached the cabins, Tracy suddenly rose up from behind one of the stumps, his rifle at the ready. A shot rang out, and one of the deputies fell. Another shot and a stifled cry revealed that a second man was wounded.

After firing a third shot at the *Seattle Times* reporter, who fell to the ground simply to fake his death, Tracy hurried off into the undergrowth, and less than a mile away was able to steal a horse to continue his journey. For the next while, he spent his time in and around the suburbs of Seattle, approaching farmers for food and occasional shelter. Descriptions of him varied. Some said he was tall. Some short. Some said he was very imposing-looking and always wore a black hat. Others maintained he was always bareheaded. His disguises and changes of clothing obviously paid off; nobody was able to positively identify the real Harry Tracy.

Tracy's next confirmed sighting was at the home of Mrs. Van Horn, a widow who lived on Phinney Avenue North in Seattle. Earlier that day, he had forced a farmer named Louis Johnson at gunpoint to drive him into Seattle in his wagon. By then, Tracy had obviously disposed of his stolen horse, and he needed some kind of transportation and a place to stop for a meal. He chose the Van Horn house because it seemed pleasant, and ordered Johnson to stop there and go inside with him.

Mrs. Van Horn recognized Tracy immediately and asked him what he wanted with her. "Food, madam, and clothing," he replied.

As it happened, Mrs. Van Horn was entertaining a Mr. Butterfield for dinner that evening, but this did not deter Tracy. He waited while she prepared a meal for them all, including Johnson, and in the meantime relieved Butterfield of his clothing. He told Mrs. Van Horn that he had never held up a lady before, and promised he would not tie her up when he left if she swore not to say anything about him being there. A brave and spunky lady, Mrs. Van Horn replied that she would only remain silent that night. "But tomorrow morning I will report you though."

Figuring he'd be far away by morning, Tracy agreed. He complimented her on her cooking, and said he hadn't enjoyed a meal that much in three years. As he ate, he conversed pleasantly, even telling her, Butterfield, and Johnson about his yachting trip from Olympia to Seattle.

When a grocery boy stopped by the house, Mrs. Van Horn went to the door with Tracy's gun pointed at her back. The criminal warned her to say nothing about his presence or it would mean her death, but she still managed to nod significantly towards the room and mouth the word *Tracy* to the boy, who set off immediately to inform Sheriff Cudihee. In no time, the relentless sheriff was lying in ambush with a posse outside Mrs. Van Horn's home.

When Tracy rose to take his departure, his instincts warned him to walk away from the house flanked on either side by Butterfield and Johnson. Although the sheriff's Winchester was aimed at the men the whole time, Cudihee decided not to fire because he wasn't sure which of the three men was Harry Tracy.

Suddenly, other members of the posse rushed out of their cover. One aimed his rifle at the men and ordered Tracy to throw down his gun. Ever the quick draw, Tracy turned and fired point-blank, killing the man instantly. Two more shots mortally wounded another of the sheriff's men. Tracy himself jumped over a nearby fence and headed for a wooded area, while Sheriff Cudihee fired shots at his retreating figure, none of which hit their mark. Once again, the elusive killer had escaped. By then, Harry Tracy's murder count within Washington State alone was nine.

He continued to roam the Puget Sound area, sometimes doubling back over the same ground, and frequently holding people at gunpoint for provisions or clothing. Although he had left behind a trail of blood and dead bodies, remarkably he remained uninjured himself, and felt no remorse for his actions; in his opinion, it had been necessary to kill in order to survive.

At the turn of the century, Puget Sound country was densely forested and offered Tracy plenty of places to hide. The bloodhounds on his trail, however, bothered him, and on one occasion he ambushed them and shot some. On another occasion, he laid poison on the ground.

In his meanderings, Tracy held up another family by the name of Johnson, took their hired help — a man named Anderson — as hostage, and then doubled back towards Seattle. Cutting around Lake Washington, he headed towards Renton, where he took shelter as the uninvited guest of the Jerold family.

Tracy came across the younger members of the Jerold family while they were picking salmonberries along the road with two other ladies. Introducing himself pleasantly, he told the group that he'd never harmed a woman in his life, and did not intend to start now. He then walked slowly back to the Jerold house with the women, tied Anderson up outside, and ordered the young Jerold boy to take two wristwatches into town and sell them so that he could buy two .45 caliber single-action Colt revolvers and a box of cartridges. Tracy warned the terrified boy that he would kill everyone in the house if the youngster betrayed him.

When the boy took off for town, Tracy turned to Mrs. Jerold. "That was merely bluff," he said. "I wouldn't hurt you. I have a mother of my own somewhere back east. I haven't done just right by her, but I reckon all mothers are safe from me, no matter what happens."

Mrs. Jerold later reported to the authorities that Tracy had tears in his eyes as he spoke, perhaps the only indication of a crack in the hard shell he had built around himself since childhood.

The events that took place in the Jerold household that evening were perhaps the most amazing of all that had happened while Harry Tracy was at large. Tracy conducted himself at all times in a gentlemanly manner, laughing and enjoying the company of the women. He offered to carry in wood for their fire and brought in water from the spring, but always with his rifle close at hand.

At one point, Tracy heard a train in the distance and remarked that there were probably more gentlemen on that train looking for him. He explained to the women that men were always coming after him. First it would be a reporter, then a cloud of dust, and after a while the deputies followed. He then complained that the stories written about him were often exaggerated and frequently misinformed. Had one not known the true events of the past few weeks and the horror that

Tracy had left in his wake, one could be excused for believing that he was simply a gentleman caller enjoying the company of ladies for a pleasant evening.

Meanwhile, the young Jerold boy had decided to take a risk. He informed the sheriff of Tracy's presence at his home, and soon a posse was heading out to the Jerold place. In no time, the sheriff and his deputies were circling the farmhouse, upsetting the ladies inside. Tracy, however, remained calm — until he noticed a photographer outside trying to take a picture of the house. Then he complained he was not suitably dressed.

"These trousers are too short and they're not nicely pressed," he quipped. "I would prefer to be better dressed for a photograph in the company of ladies." Smirking, he threatened to kill one of the deputies outside and steal his trousers.

Time passed, and one of the ladies remarked that she was worried she would not be home before dark. Tracy tried to reassure her by saying that the moon would be very bright that night. He also promised that if he were able, he would even see her safely home himself.

The deputies, meanwhile, kept up their vigil around the house, all the time getting closer and closer. Tracy realized it was time to leave. He thanked his hostess for her kind hospitality and headed for the back door.

As luck would have it, at the very moment Tracy

was about to leave, one of the deputies shouted that he had found Anderson, who was still tied to the tree where Tracy had left him. This temporary distraction allowed Tracy just enough time to slip quietly away towards the river, where once again he disappeared into the night.

And so the chase continued. For days Tracy played "cat and mouse" with his pursuers throughout King County. On one occasion he even made a telephone call to Sheriff Cudihee, complimenting him on his thoroughness. "You've done much better than the other sheriffs," he said. "And at least you can say that you have now actually talked with the man you are searching for." He then bade the sheriff farewell, adding, "You won't see me again I'm afraid."

Soon after making that call, Tracy left the cover of the Cascades and headed towards Eastern Washington on horseback. (Often when he stole a horse, he would later release it so that it returned to its owner.) Some people believed he was making for his old stomping ground in Wyoming to seek help from his criminal cronies there. A few members of the old gang were still around and would be willing to hide him from the authorities.

Unfortunately for Tracy, Eastern Washington did not offer as much cover as he had found in the west. Modern telegraph wires were constantly updating his

progress from place to place. In addition, Sheriff
Cudihee, now in company with Sheriffs Gardner and
Doust, was more determined than ever to bring Harry
Tracy to justice.

* * *

By the time Tracy reached the Eddy ranch near Creston
in early August, he had become a cold, bitter man
sapped of all his physical strength. Nonetheless, he
remained as dangerous as the day he had first broken
out of the penitentiary, and he had left many dead bodies behind him to prove it.

Tracy still refused to come quietly, even when surrounded by a five-man posse led by Sheriffs Gardner
and Cudihee. Upon spotting the officers, he quickly
jumped behind farmer Eddy and the team of horses he
had been about to unhitch. Then, using the terrified
farmer as cover, Tracy ordered Eddy to back up towards
the barn so that he could retrieve his rifle. Having
accomplished this and now feeling more secure, he
headed off away from the posse.

Hiding behind a haystack and then a nearby boul-
der as he darted away, Tracy fired shot after shot at the
pursuing officers, but the sun in his eyes caused him to
shoot off target. One returning shot from the posse

caught him in the leg, splintering his shinbone and sev-
ering an artery. He then managed to crawl into a nearby
wheat field, still shooting wildly as he lay in agony on his
back.

Tracy now realized the hopelessness of his situation. It was worse than any he had encountered along
the way, but he had vowed long ago never to be taken
alive again. So, slowly placing the revolver to his forehead, he fired his last bullet, the one that sent him into
eternity. One of the most amazing manhunts in
Washington State history had finally come to an end.

But even after that last shot rang out in the wheat
field, Tracy's pursuers still could not believe he was really dead. They had become so wary of this manipulative
killer that they doubted he would actually die by his own
hand. Was it a trick? They decided to wait until daybreak
before advancing any further.

At dawn, they slowly walked into the field and
found the lifeless body of Harry Tracy. It was true. He
was indeed dead, and he had died by his own bullet.

Tracy's remains were then removed to the nearby
town of Davenport, where the townsfolk gathered
around in a frenzy, trying to strip off his shoes and tear
at his clothes in order to obtain souvenirs. Everyone
wanted something that had belonged to the most notorious killer Washington State had ever known. Pieces of

his hair were cut off, and his guns were fought over. For years afterwards, the gags and ropes he had used to hold his hostages were considered prized mementos by those who still had them, as was the actual gun he had used to end his own life.

And even when Harry Tracy's body was safely placed inside a simple pine box to be transported to the Oregon State Penitentiary for burial, crowds began to hack at it with axes and knives in order to retrieve splinters of wood as souvenirs.

Harry Tracy, Public Enemy Number One, was finally gone — but his legend refused to die.

Chapter 4
The Carpenter
and the Violinist

ames William (Bill) Byrd of Spokane led an exemplary life — exemplary, that is, until he killed three men and was sent to Walla Walla Prison for murder. Described as "a common laborer with the skills of a talented carpenter," 38-year-old Byrd was Catholic, unmarried, and a good son to his mother. He had one brother and one sister, and his father had died just a few weeks prior to the incident that changed his entire life.

It all began on June 8, 1911, when Byrd decided it was time to settle a score with his ex-employers, William Mansker and George Whipple. Byrd claimed the men still owed him money, and asked them to meet him at a

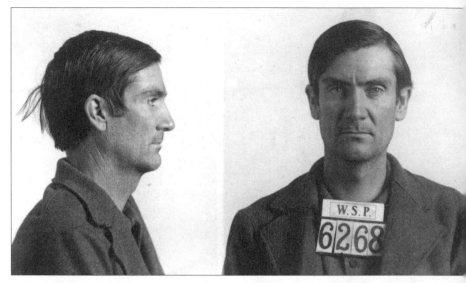

Mug shots of Bill Byrd

nearby barbershop to settle up. When they did not show, he found out they were working on a building in the Dishman area of Spokane and decided to pay them a visit. After taking a drink for courage, he headed out to the construction site — with a gun.

Byrd later stated that he had only intended to use the gun as a deterrent. Mankster and Whipple, however, made disparaging remarks to Byrd and began throwing hammers and hatchets at him. Then, producing revolvers of their own, they ordered him to leave the construction site and threatened to kill him if he did not. In a fit of anger, Byrd loaded his gun and started shooting at the men, killing them both in what he claimed was self-defense.

A group of law enforcers was quickly formed to chase Byrd as he fled the scene. They fired at least 35 shots at him before Byrd pleaded with them to stop shooting. When they refused, he fired one shot back, which unfortunately killed a third man, Charles Misner, who was also a justice of the peace. Byrd was captured several days later at a nearby farmhouse where he'd been hiding. He was arrested and charged with murder in the first degree.

In October of 1911, Byrd was tried and convicted of murder in the second degree by a jury that claimed he'd had some provocation for his actions. He was sentenced to imprisonment in the state penitentiary at Walla Walla for a term of not less than 35 or more than 45 years. His lawyers later argued that the minimum should have been 10 years. Byrd's sentence began on November 4, 1911.

The Washington State Penitentiary at Walla Walla was constructed in 1886, built on land donated by the citizens of the area. The prison's first inmates took up residency in 1887. Consisting mostly of hardened criminals, these prisoners were forced to shave their heads and don striped prison-issue uniforms. Soon, the men grew to resemble one another, all wearing a similar expression of hopelessness. After spending several years there, Byrd came to realize that he, like many of the other embittered inmates, could still be touched by beauty despite his dismal environment. This realization came in the 1920s, when his path crossed with that of a talented Russian-born violinist named Esther Sundquist Bowers.

At the time of Bill Byrd's conviction, Esther Sundquist was still a teenager with a passion for music. Despite being born blind, with cataracts covering both of her eyes, Esther had developed a love and a feel for playing the violin. She had spent her childhood years in pre-revolutionary Russia. Her family's home was situated across the street from the Tsar's Winter Palace in St. Petersburg.

It was a dangerous time to be living in Russia, and spies were everywhere. When authorities found pictures in Esther's home of her father's two cousins, both of whom were suspected Nihilists, a guard was posted at the family's back door and the seal of the Tsar was placed over the front door, making it impossible for her father to leave. Authorities made it known that they intended to investigate his connection to the cousins, and in the meantime, he became a prisoner in his own home.

Nihilists were members of a political organization

working against the aristocracy, and they were gaining many supporters among all classes of society. Their work was carried out in secret, but they were thought to be involved in the growing conspiracies and assassinations in Russia. In 1881, it was believed that Nihilists were responsible for the assassination of Tsar Alexander II. Anyone who supported or sympathized with Nihilism was considered dangerous in the eyes of the ruling aristocracy.

Esther's family, however, had many friends, all of whom helped her father escape. They plied the guard at the back door with vodka until he was completely drunk, at which point her father was able to slip away from the house, disappearing into the night by lying on the rails of a moving garbage sled. He then ice-skated across the Niva River to safety in Finland, where he changed his name from Petil to Sundquist. Eventually, he took a steamer to America, and once in Chicago was offered a job with an Opera Company because of his powerful baritone voice. As soon as he had saved enough money, he sent for his wife and children.

Esther's mother brought her children to New York, entering the New World through Ellis Island. When immigration officers noticed that six-year-old Esther's unseeing eyes were covered in bandages, they feared the child might have some sort of communicable disease, and they moved the Sundquist family to one side. But Esther's mother was a determined woman, and she was not about to be sent back after she had come so far. Once the authorities were occupied with another group of immigrants, she led her children quietly away, mixing with another family who was passing through the barriers. Finally, she was safely in America and reunited with her husband. Soon, the family was on its way to Chicago.

After a successful operation, Esther gained sight in one eye and was able to pursue her earlier passion for music. She took violin lessons at the Chicago Musical College, where she received the Gold Medal of Merit in 1905, which was presented to her by Flo Ziegfeld's father, who was president of the college at that time. Eventually she joined the class of the famous Leopold Auer, and soon became an incredibly accomplished violinist.

Following the death of her father, Esther's family moved to Astoria, Oregon, where her mother ran a boarding house. However, shortly after the move, Esther's mother also died, and Esther, though still in her teens, had to hold down three jobs to support and feed her siblings. Times were tough for the Sundquist family.

One of Esther's jobs was on the vaudeville stage, where she became so popular that audiences lined up outside theaters to see her. On many occasions, she received standing ovations before she even raised her bow to play. Her presence on stage was magical, full of passion and emotion. She connected with her audience members, and they responded in kind. Once, she was even asked by Minnie Madern Fiske (the Helen Hayes of her day) to come back with her to Broadway, where Minnie would make her a star. But by then, Esther had met a gentleman by the name of George Bowers.

Mr. Bowers had accompanied a friend to the theater one night to see Esther perform because the friend had promised him she was exceptional. Bowers had already had a date lined up for that evening, but the lady in question had become sick. So, somewhat reluctantly, he had agreed to go out with his friend instead.

From the moment he first saw Esther, George knew he was in love. He became a "stage-door Johnny," hanging around the theater and adoring Esther from afar until he was able to convince her to allow him to court her officially. Their courtship led to marriage in September of 1914. When they married, George not only gained a wife, he also took in Esther's three youngest siblings,and the five of them moved out to his ranch outside Walla Walla, Washington.

In the past, Esther's paychecks had always gone to support her siblings, so when she first married George and went to live on his ranch, she had no ordinary housedresses to wear. She only owned stage costumes, and until she was able to buy other dresses, she would often be seen feeding the chickens in the evening gowns she wore for her performances.

When the family eventually moved back into town, Esther began giving private violin lessons, and held a position in the Music Department at Whitman College. There, she had her own studio and also conducted the college orchestra. Esther was a member of a string quartet as well, and she directed a church choir. On summer nights, many of the Walla Walla townsfolk were treated to free concerts as Esther walked up and down the street practicing her violin. During this time, Esther also began to give special concerts for the inmates at Walla Walla prison.

And so it was that Bill Byrd had the opportunity to see Esther Sundquist Bowers perform. Like so many before him, he became enchanted by her presence, her exquisite beauty, and her music. He desperately wanted to show his appreciation for all the pleasure she brought to him and the other men in prison. When they listened to her beautiful music, the prisoners were able to escape the confines of the prison walls for a while, and travel to some imaginary, far off place of beauty. The men all particularly enjoyed her rendition of "Nobody Knows

The Trouble I've Seen," which usually brought down the house.

For 11 years, Byrd had been a model prisoner, and under normal circumstances, he would by then have been eligible for parole. Numerous people had written letters of recommendation to the governor on Byrd's behalf. There had even been a letter from Mrs. Blanche Smith, the sister of Charles Misner (the third man that Byrd had shot). She believed that the incident had simply been a slip in character on Byrd's part, a misjudgment in the heat of the moment, due perhaps to Byrd having taken a drink that day. She had studied the case well and understood that her brother had faced the risk of being killed simply because of his job.

Byrd's brother John, as well as his mother and her lawyer, had also written letters to the governor. But, despite having an exemplary prison record and the support of numerous people who begged that he be pardoned on the grounds of his mother's failing health, Byrd was continually refused parole. He stayed behind bars.

No one knows for sure what Byrd suffered while he was incarcerated, or how much he might have regretted his actions back in June of 1911. It is obvious, however, that the concerts given by Esther Sundquist Bowers made life more bearable for him. In 1923, still wanting to repay her in some way, Byrd asked the warden for permission to make her two wooden boxes. These boxes were so well crafted, and made with such incredible skill and love, that Esther was quite overwhelmed by her treasured gifts. The larger of the two, which was hope-chest size, was crafted with thousands of inlaid pieces of wood, while the smaller one contained at least a thousand pieces made from various different woods.

The warden was also impressed, and in 1925, he ordered Byrd to make a chest for the prison chaplain. Once again, the chest was skillfully built, and was said to have contained 48,600 pieces of wood. The chaplain was later offered $5000 for it.

For some unknown reason, after Byrd had completed the chest, his woodworking tools were taken from him and he was locked up in solitary confinement, where he remained for 18 months. During that time he was allowed no visitors or mail, and his requests for parole went unanswered.

When Byrd finally came up for parole again in January of 1927, it was discovered that the warden had mentioned in passing that as long as *he* was warden at Walla Walla Prison, Byrd would never be paroled or released. Charles Misner had been a close friend of his and, because of that, he was determined that Byrd would pay the price. This remark was overheard by a number of people around the time of Byrd's 1927 parole hearing, and it is believed that it became the reason why Byrd's parole was finally granted.

Bill Byrd was at last released, and in 1932, at the age of 59, he was granted complete discharge. He had spent 21 years behind bars, several of which had been made more bearable by the joy of hearing Esther play her violin.

Years later, the larger of the two boxes that Byrd crafted for Esther was destroyed in a house fire, but the smaller one is still the treasured possession of Esther's daughter in Seattle. The inscription inside reads as follows: "To Mrs. Esther Sundquist Bowers, in grateful appreciation of the happiness she brings to the men behind the walls, and to convey the assurance that her beautiful music has lightened the burdens for all the inmates of the Washington State Penitentiary."

Esther Sundquist Bowers died in 1969 in Seattle, never having revealed her true age to any member of her family. And, in time, the story of how a prisoner's life was enriched by their famous Russian ancestor became a Sundquist-Bowers family legend.

Chapter 5
Marriage, Money, and Murder

n February 10, 1921, 38-year-old James E. Mahoney stood before a justice of the peace in the King County Courthouse and became the fourth husband of 72-year-old Kate Mooers. Not only was their union strange because of the great age difference. It was also illegal.

Mahoney already had a wife tucked away, and was therefore committing bigamy when he married Kate. Of course, he wasn't breaking the law for love; his motives for marrying the older woman were far less noble — it was all about money. Kate Mooers was a very wealthy woman. She owned a great deal of real estate in Seattle and had a number of large bank accounts. In her own way, the older woman was quite a catch.

But what could she have possibly seen in her young husband? A surly man with no apparent pleasant side, Mahoney was an ex-con who had served time for burglary and was now on parole. Indeed, he was far from typically good marriage material. Then again, the other marriages Kate Mooers had entered into had also been unusual unions — though each had left her considerably wealthier. Years before, under the name Kate Keeler, she had accumulated a large fortune in Butte, Montana, from her first husband. Later, at the age of 45, and then using the name Wyant from a second marriage (about which little is known), she married for the third time in Vancouver, Washington. That time she had chosen a young man of only 19, who later became a physician of note. In August of 1919, when trying to obtain his freedom in an amicable divorce from his now aging wife, he deeded to her all his Seattle properties, valued at $75,000, plus some gold mining claims in Alaska and a 270-acre farm in Texas.

By then, Kate also owned a $4000 ranch in Oregon, and in 1916, she had been left $10,000 in her sister's will. At the time of her marriage to James Mahoney, her total wealth was estimated to be in excess of $100,000, and was probably nearer to $200,000. She also owned a safe deposit box, the contents of which were known only to her. Mahoney later made it his business to find out what the box contained, but he already suspected it would be something of value, bearing in mind all her other assets.

His decision to marry Kate had come about through desperation, as he had been having great difficulty finding work. Prior to his prison sentence, he had worked for the Great Northern Railway. Once out on parole, he had reapplied for a job there, only to discover that many men were being laid off and there was nothing suitable for him. He had then found work as a supply buyer and general agent for the Washington Fertilizer Company. But he'd also applied for a job with another company, one that had offered him free transportation to California and a position there in the orange crop business, a line of work that was very lucrative at that time. Mahoney had pleaded with his parole officer for permission to leave Washington temporarily so that he could make money in California and then return to Seattle after the summer, once the railway business picked up. Permission was delayed and, in the meantime, Mahoney had met Kate and decided that she would be his meal ticket instead. Wasting no time, he cancelled his to plans to leave Washington and proposed to his new, elderly lady friend.

A month before the wedding, Mahoney had written to his parole officer asking for permission to marry. He'd wanted to make sure he was not violating his parole, and that everything would be above board. He was told there was no law against marrying while on parole, but was advised that it might be preferable to wait until he was a completely free man. However, if he decided to go ahead — which of course he did — he was wished good luck and the hope that the marriage "would be wholly beneficial to both yourself and your partner."

A few weeks after the wedding, Mahoney realized he had married a skinflint. The first thing Kate did was cut him out of her will. Then she put him on a very small daily allowance, which both humiliated and angered him. By April of 1921, he decided he'd had enough of her miserly ways.

That's when he came up with a plan. He purchased some poison and fed it to his unsuspecting wife. Though the poison killed Kate quickly, Mahoney nonetheless hit her over the head with a hammer to be sure she was dead, and then stuffed her lifeless body into a steamer trunk. Disposal of the trunk, though, proved harder than he expected.

At first, Mahoney wanted to dump the trunk and its grisly contents into Lake Washington, but boat rentals there were too expensive for him. After some searching, he found a boat rental company at Lake Union whose prices were more affordable. He then hired a transport company to carry the heavy trunk from his home to the lake. Later that night, he rowed his rented boat out to the middle of the lake and heaved the trunk into the water.

But the trunk would not sink! It simply floated on the waves. Frustrated, Mahoney tried to figure out his next move. He wanted that trunk safely at the bottom of the lake where it would never be found. Not knowing what else to do, he decided to risk rowing back to shore, where he remembered seeing several large pieces of concrete. After placing these pieces inside the trunk, he rowed back to the middle of the lake. By then he was exhausted, and the boat was getting lower and lower in the water and leaking badly. So, it was with great relief that he heaved the trunk overboard again, and this time watched it sink.

Mahoney knew he would need an explanation for his wife's disappearance, so he concocted a story. But first he forged her signature on a power of attorney form, enabling him to get into her safe deposit box. To his delight, the box contained a number of bonds, which he promptly cashed. He then boarded a train to St. Paul, Minnesota, in the company of a woman friend who wore her coat collar high up around her face and traveled under the name "Mrs. Mahoney."

Once in St. Paul, he wrote a letter on hotel

stationery to Kate's family back home, pretending to be her. The family was immediately suspicious because the content of the letter was very unlike Kate, and the hand-writing seemed different. The authorities were soon notified, and an investigation into Kate's disappearance began under the jurisdiction of Chief Charles Tennant, a detective with the Seattle Police Department who was determined to get to the bottom of the mystery.

In the middle of all this, James Mahoney made the mistake of returning to Seattle. He told everyone that he and Kate had quarreled in St. Paul, and that she had decided to travel abroad alone. But by this time, Tennant had discovered the forged power of attorney. Not believing a word of Mahoney's story, Tennant arrest-ed him on charges of forgery and held him in jail pend-ing further investigation.

The boat rental and truck hauling companies soon came forward and reported that a man resembling Mahoney had done business with them recently. Now Tennant was more determined than ever to discover Kate's whereabouts. On a hunch, he ordered that Lake Union be dragged inch by inch. On May 25, this decision made headlines in *The Seattle & Daily Times*. While Mahoney sat in jail on forgery charges, Tennant was telling news reporters, "We are dragging the Lake believ-ing we may find a body connected to the Mahoney case."

But James Mahoney stuck to his original story and refused to budge. He swore that he and his "bride" had left for St. Paul on April 18 for a belated honeymoon, that he had returned after they'd quarreled, and that she had gone abroad alone. Insisting she would be home in June, he also claimed that his wife had willingly given him power of attorney over her affairs while she was away.

It was this claim that made Chief Tennant even more suspicious. The power of attorney had granted Mahoney jurisdiction over all of Kate's Seattle properties, and he had immediately installed his sister, Mrs. Dolores Johnson, in one of Kate's apartments, and his mother, Nora Mahoney, as manager of another apartment block. Why, Tennant wondered, would this changeover in power have taken place so quickly if Kate Mahoney was expected to return in June?

Meanwhile, Kate Mahoney's niece, Kate Stewart, continued to believe that something unpleasant had happened to her aunt. Even though reports began to surface that Kate Mahoney had been seen in various places on a number of occasions, her niece believed, just as did Charles Tennant did, that there had been foul play and that James Mahoney was responsible.

Time went on, and the lake dragging continued. Tennant was criticized for wasting the taxpayers'

James Mahoney, caught by the tenacity of Police Chief Tennant

money, but he refused to give up. Instinctively, he knew that Mahoney was guilty of more than just forgery.

On August 8, 1921, Tennant's suspicions proved correct. The trunk containing Kate Mahoney's remains bobbed to the surface of Lake Union on its own. This was probably due to the fact that the lake was not very deep, and the gases from the decomposed body had accumulated in the trunk, causing it to rise from its resting place.

Tennant was ecstatic and immediately indicted Mahoney for first-degree murder. The trial was set for September 21, and made national news when it began. A mere 10 days later, a jury found Mahoney guilty and recommended the death sentence.

His execution was set for December 1, 1922. While he waited on death row, the determined Mahoney still refused to admit his guilt. He continued to profess that he'd had nothing to do with Kate's death. Although a man resembling Mahoney was known to have rented a boat and a truck, no one could positively identify him, and Mahoney continued to maintain that he knew nothing about his wife's death.

Tennant was frustrated that he could not get a confession from Mahoney. This frustration grew as the execution date drew nearer. Others also began to worry that there might have been a miscarriage of justice. No one relished the thought of hanging an innocent man.

Then, quite unexpectedly, on the very eve of his execution, Mahoney finally decided to unburden his soul. He admitted everything, telling the whole gruesome story of how he had poisoned his tight-fisted wife and placed her body in the trunk. He said that he had murdered her in order to gain access to her money.

"But what made you chose Lake Union to dispose of the trunk?" his interrogators asked. "Lake Washington is much larger and deeper and would have been a much better choice."

Mahoney smirked. "Well, of course I went there first to try and rent a boat but they wanted $25. My wife was so cheap and she gave me only a small allowance every day, so by the time I had paid for a transport company in advance, I only had $10 left. I had to go to Lake Union where the boat rental was cheaper."

The next morning, Mahoney walked out to the courtyard of Walla Walla Prison for his meeting with the hangman. Having finally told the truth, he was now ready to meet his destiny with a modicum of dignity.

In the final analysis, Kate Mahoney's miserly ways had been her husband's downfall, and in a way had solved the case. By allowing her husband only a small amount of money each day, she had unknowingly contributed to justice finally being served when her decomposed body floated to the surface of Lake Union.

After all, had she provided her husband with a more generous allowance, her body might have been lost forever in the depths of Lake Washington, and Mahoney would have walked free.

Chapter 6
Two Gruesome Murderers

f ever there were a reason to exercise caution when placing an advertisement in a newspaper, it would be to avoid what happened to James Bassett in August of 1928. That summer, Bassett left his home in Maryland and headed west in his new Chrysler roadster. When he reached Seattle, he decided to sell the car, as he would soon be leaving the country to take a job in the Philippines.

Bassett placed an advertisement in a Seattle newspaper and received an immediate response from a couple who claimed they lived in the Richland Highlands area. The couple told Bassett they wanted to buy his car, and asked if he would drive out to meet them so they could arrange the deal. Bassett, who was anxious to begin his new life, saw nothing amiss in this request and agreed to meet the couple at an appointed place. It proved to be a deadly mistake.

The two prospective buyers were Decasto Earl Mayer, an ex-convict and career criminal with a multitude of aliases, and Mary Smith, an older woman who claimed to be Mayer's mother. Like Mayer, Smith had a number of aliases, including Ella Mary Smith, Mrs. French, and Eleanor Smith. She was known to police as "shoe-box Mary," a woman who had a habit of picking up younger men to help her look for houses and other buildings that they could later burglarize. It is unclear why she was called shoe-box Mary, but one theory speculates the records she kept of her young men were filed in a shoebox.

Smith appeared to adore Mayer, seeing no wrong in any of his past illegal activities. In her opinion, he always was and always would be the perfect son. Some people, however, believed that Mayer was not her son at all, but simply another of her "young men." And because of her track record, they had every reason to doubt her claim to motherhood.

Indeed, "shoe-box Mary" was somewhat of an enigma. What is certain about Smith and Mayer, however, is that after their meeting with James Bassett in

Seattle, they fled Washington State. One month later, the pair was arrested in Oakland, California, while driving Bassett's roadster, which had been reported stolen in Seattle by people who knew Bassett and were concerned about him.

Mayer and Smith both denied stealing the car, claiming to have purchased it from Bassett for the sum of $1600. As they continued to swear their innocence, a silver wristwatch, a set of cufflinks, and a billfold containing $25 were found in Mayer's possession. These items were identified as Bassett's, and Mayer and Smith were promptly charged with grand larceny. But the authorities were also looking to charge them with a much more serious offense — murder. James Bassett was nowhere to be found in Seattle, and he had not arrived in the Philippines to take up his new post there. He was reported missing.

One of the largest searches to date for a missing person in Washington State then took place. Lakes were scoured, and bloodhounds were brought in to search the wild bush areas close to where Bassett had last been seen. Volunteers were called in to help the police with the search in and around the Seattle area, and psychics were hired to tell them where to dig.

Despite all these efforts, Bassett's remains could not be found and, without evidence of a body, no charges of murder could be laid. Only the charge of grand larceny of an automobile would stick against the 31-year-old Mayer and the middle-aged Smith, and after a speedy trial, the two were found guilty. Smith was sentenced to 10 years in prison, and her son was given life.

The sentencing seemed stiff for grand larceny — until one considered the past crimes of these two characters. Decasto Earl Mayer had been in trouble with the law for most of his life, and since 1917 had spent a great deal of time in jail on charges ranging from theft to being involved in the white slave trade. His many aliases included Earl Decasto Mayer, E. Clark, C.D. Montaigne, C.C. Skidmore, D.E. Montague, D.E. Montaigne, C.C. Skedmore, and Earl Montague.

Mary Smith's past was equally grim. Born in Pennsylvania in 1865, she left home at the age of 18, began associating with unsavory characters, and was soon involved in various burglaries. She always claimed to be a hard-working traveling saleswoman, and although she had no previous prison record at the time of her arrest and sentencing, her questionable history prompted authorities to punish her accordingly.

And so the unlikely couple served their time in the penitentiary. Each time Mary Smith came before the parole board, her parole was denied, and it was recommended that she serve her full term, which would not end until May 9, 1938. As the years went by, the Mayer/Smith case was all but forgotten. Neither inmate appeared to cause much trouble in prison, though both were frequently called up on minor offenses. On one occasion, Mayer was reprimanded for hiding an electric iron in his cell. Other offenses included falling out of place in line and working in the machine shop without permission. Smith was called up a number of times for "disregarding the rules."

Then, 10 years after mother and son were first handed their sentences, their story became front-page news all over again. It appeared that Mary Smith had grown extremely bored behind bars and had started talking to one of her fellow inmates, a swindler by the name of Margaret Fawcett. One day, the two women were comparing their past crimes, and Smith, knowing she could easily outdo Fawcett, described the events that really took place in August of 1928. Smith told Fawcett about the man whose car she and her son had stolen. She confided that she and her son had then murdered Bassett, and that her son had dismembered his body in the bathtub while she cleaned up the mess. She then went on to explain that her poor son had been so exhausted after chopping Bassett's body into pieces that she'd had to fix him an eggnog to help him regain his

The boastful Mary Smith

strength. Soon after, they had buried the body parts in four different areas of King County.

Fascinated by the lurid details of Smith's story, Fawcett decided to repeat it to the warden. Naturally, the warden was astounded by the tale and quickly contacted the police. Knowing that hearsay evidence would not be admissible in court, the authorities realized they needed to come up with another plan to make Smith talk again. The plan they agreed upon was completely unethical, but at the time it seemed like a brilliant idea. They had an undercover policeman visit Smith in her cell dressed as a priest. While he was there, the "priest" suggested that Smith admit all her past crimes to him so that her soul could be unburdened and she could rest peacefully in her declining years. He promised that everything she told him would be kept in confidence.

Despite never having been a religious woman, Mary Smith prayed with the very convincing priest, and finally admitted to murdering Bassett. Of course, this confession would still prove a problem in court, and the police knew it. It would not stand up as legitimate evidence, so the next step was to bring Mary Smith and Decasto Earl Mayer together for further interrogation, playing one against the other in the hopes of getting a confession from them both.

But somehow, Mayer got wind of Smith's talk with the "priest" and decided to cheat the authorities by hanging himself in his cell the night before he was due to be interrogated. The authorities then agreed that there seemed little point in interrogating Smith further, so she was returned to her cell to serve out her time.

Mary Smith was released back into society in May of 1938, having by then served her maximum sentence for grand larceny. By the end of that same year, however, she was re-arrested on "suspicion of murder" by police, who had been keeping a close eye on her. This time, the 73-year-old woman confessed to her crimes. She was found guilty of first-degree murder and sentenced to life. Shoe-box Mary was back in the slammer!

In March of 1953, at the age of 88, her life sentence was considered to have been served, and she was released on parole. She spent many more years on earth, finally passing away in a Seattle nursing home at the ripe old age of 100.

If Mary Smith had any conscience at all, her true punishment was having had to live for so many more years with the memory of what she and Mayer had done to an innocent man who merely wanted to sell his car.

Chapter 7
The Real Butch Cassidy?

o this day, Robert LeRoy Parker (better known as Butch Cassidy) remains one of the most notorious and charismatic outlaws of the American Wild West. But his death also continues to be one of the West's greatest mysteries. Did he really die in a 1908 shootout in San Vincente, Bolivia, or did his death occur almost 30 years years later in Spokane, Washington?

Historians, writers, researchers, and history buffs have pondered this question for decades. The theory that Cassidy faked his death in South America, escaped to France, had plastic surgery, and then reinvented himself as William Thadeus Phillips of Spokane is a possibility that no one has ever been able to completely dismiss. It is the ultimate unsolved mystery.

In 1908, Butch Cassidy and his partner Harry Longabaugh (the Sundance Kid) virtually disappeared off the face of the earth, though their deaths were not widely reported until the 1930s. Longabaugh's family was inclined to believe that he did die in South America, but some members of Cassidy's family believed that Butch survived the shootout and died much later.

Through the years, assorted versions of the pair's demise surfaced and multiplied around the world. Did both outlaws die in Bolivia, or did Butch Cassidy actually die in Vernal in the 1920s? Or was it in Oregon in 1930? Or Mexico in 1932? Or, could it be that, using the name William Thadeus Phillips, he died in Spokane in 1937? This last possibility is certainly the most intriguing of all the "where-did-Butch-Cassidy-really-die?" theories.

If Butch Cassidy and William Thadeus Phillips were indeed one and the same, then the story of Mr. Phillips begins on April 13, 1866, in Beaver, Utah, where Robert Leroy Parker was born and raised. His father ran a general store in Beaver for several years, but in 1879 the Parkers moved their growing family to a ranch near Circleville, an area well known as a hangout for outlaws.

It was there that young Robert developed a hero worship for an unsavory character named Mike Cassidy, who gave the teenager his first saddle and a gun. At age 16, Robert left home to become second-in-command to Mike Cassidy's cattle rustling outfit. Eventually, the pair moved on into Wyoming, where they met up with a group of men who later became members of the Wild Bunch gang in Hole-in-the-Wall Country.

In 1887, Robert took part in a train robbery in Colorado, and two years later was keeping busy robbing banks in Denver and Telluride. By then, he was going by the name "George Cassidy." When he returned to Wyoming and found honest work in a butcher's shop in Rock Springs, he adopted the nickname "Butch."

Over the years, Butch Cassidy often tried to go straight. He worked on various ranches as a cowboy, and searched for other legitimate jobs as well. However, by the 1890s he was back to cattle rustling, and in 1892 he was arrested and taken into custody for the first time. His trial was delayed until 1894, at which time he was sentenced to serve two years in the Wyoming State Penitentiary.

Following his release in 1896, Cassidy returned to a life of crime. He began by forming the notorious Wild Bunch gang with criminals such as Harvey Logan, Harry Longabaugh, Ben Kilpatrick, Elzy Lay, Harry Tracy, and Big Nose George Curry. During the following years, Cassidy and the Wild Bunch successfully robbed a number of trains and banks. They made a great deal of money at their trade, enabling them to live the good life between heists. Cassidy was also a ladies' man. He enjoyed the company of many women, including his long-time sweetheart, Mary Boyd.

By 1900, however, all the good times were coming to an end; the law was closing in on Cassidy and his gang of outlaws. In 1902, after never having been able to settle in one place for long, Cassidy and Longabaugh, together with Longabaugh's mistress, Etta Place, decided to head for South America to try to make an honest living. On the way, they stopped in New York for an extended holiday. Cassidy parted company with Longabaugh and Place while there,but agreed to meet up with them in Montevideo, Uruguay. From Uruguay, the trio went on to Argentina to operate a cattle and sheep ranch, trailing their herds into Chile and making a profitable and honest living.

But by 1907, the two outlaws had returned to their old activities, and were robbing banks in Bolivia. It seemed that the thrill of a life of crime was in their blood, and it was hard to change the habits of a lifetime.

Although there are several accounts of what actually happened in Bolivia, it appears that early in 1908, Bolivian soldiers cornered the two outlaws and a shootout ensued. In one version of the story,

Longabaugh was shot and killed, but Cassidy escaped by faking his own death. Cassidy then made his way back to the United States via France, where he underwent plastic surgery in Paris.

Meanwhile, records of a gentleman by the name of William Thadeus Phillips first materialized in Spokane in 1911. Phillips's name appears in a city street directory from that year, where he was listed as vice-president of the America Stereo Typewriter Company. He claimed to be a mechanical engineer from Des Moines, Iowa, and stated that in May of 1908, he had married Gertrude Livesay in Adrian, Michigan. He also claimed to have spent some time across the border as a mercenary in the Mexican Revolution — the sort of adventure that Butch Cassidy would have enjoyed.

By 1910, Mr. and Mrs. Phillips had moved to Spokane, and within five years, Phillips had established The Phillips Manufacturing Company, a business that specialized in producing adding machines and other business equipment. The company prospered, and Phillips appeared to be a model citizen. He became a member of the Elks and of the Masons, and indulged his hobby of buying fine automobiles (just as Butch Cassidy had always indulged his passion for owning the finest horses). In 1919, the childless couple adopted a son, who they called William Richard, and by 1925, the

Phillips family was living on Providence Avenue in an elegant home they had purchased for $5000.

It is a matter of record that William Thadeus Phillips lived in Spokane from 1910 until his death in 1937, but it is also known as fact that in the years 1925, 1930, 1934, and 1936, he visited places in Wyoming where he was recognized as Butch Cassidy. If Phillips was an impostor, he certainly was a good one because he fooled a number of his old acquaintances, even his old sweetheart, Mary Boyd Rhodes, who was now a widow. He supposedly resumed an affair with her during those years. Many of these old friends claimed in later interviews that they had known Butch Cassidy too well to have been taken in by an impostor.

It is believed that on those trips to Wyoming, Phillips might also have been looking for "loot" that had been hidden back in the Wild Bunch days. By 1934, the Depression was hurting businesses everywhere. Phillips's company had gone bankrupt, and he was desperate for money.

It was then that he came up with the idea of writing a manuscript, which he later titled *The Bandit Invincible*. The story, written in the third person, described Butch Cassidy's life leading up to his faked death in South America. Phillips explained to suspicious friends and acquaintances that he had once known

Cassidy, and was therefore very familiar with the events of his life. He tried desperately to have the manuscript published, but was never successful.

According to the *Encyclopedia of Western Gunfighters* by Bill O'Neal, Phillips also came up with a plan to kidnap a wealthy Spokane resident for ransom, but never carried it through. Perhaps he had lost his old "Butch Cassidy" touch, or it could have been because by then he was in failing health and no longer had the inclination to make money — legally or illegally. Phillips had developed cancer, which, within months, caused his death in 1937 at Broadacres, the county poor farm in Spangle.

His inconspicuous obituary, which appeared in *The Spokane Review*, read:

Funeral Services for William T. Phillips, age 72, consulting engineer and notably known for the bridges he built during his 27 years of residence in Spokane, will be held tonight at 7:30 in the Alwin Chapel, Hazen & Jaegar's. Rose Croix services will be conducted, with incineration following.

Mr. Phillips, a member of Oriental lodge 74, F & A.M. and the Scottish Rite bodies, is survived by his widow, Gertrude, at their home on W828 Glass, and a son, William Richard Phillips, also of Spokane.

The Real Butch Cassidy?

Forty years after Phillips's death, his son William was interviewed by reporter Mike Schmeltzer for an article in *The Spokane Review*. In the interview, William stated that he believed his father was indeed Butch Cassidy, and that it had been a "family secret" which his mother had shared with him when he was a young man of 20. He also recalled how, as a child, he would go up to bed and pretend to be asleep, but would really be listening to his father's voice downstairs as he talked to close friends about the train and bank robberies that he had taken part in as a young man. According to William, his father only shared those stories with friends he trusted.

Back in 1938, Gertrude Phillips had denied to reporters that her husband was Butch Cassidy. She did admit, however, that he had once known Cassidy years earlier, explaining — as her husband had before her — that that was how he'd been able to write *The Bandit Invincible* with such knowledge and conviction. According to William, his mother's denial was made simply to spare her the embarrassment and notoriety that the truth would have brought them. She did not want that kind of publicity to plague her or her son for the rest of their lives.

But if Gertrude had been telling the truth that Phillips was not Butch Cassidy, then who was he? His death certificate stated that he was born on June 22,

1865, but it does not say where. On his application to join the Elks, he stated he was born in Sandusky, Michigan, and listed his parents as Laddie J. and Cecilia Mudge Phillips. However, the town of Sandusky was not founded until 1870, and investigators later discovered that there is no record of a William T. Phillips having even been born in that area in 1865. There is also no evidence of a Cecilia or Laddie Phillips living or owning property there at that time.

In addition, Gertrude had once stated that her husband had owned a machine shop in Des Moines before their marriage, and had worked on buildings in New York. No trace was ever found of the Des Moines business. Indeed, it seemed there was no evidence that a William T. Phillips even existed prior to his marriage to Gertrude Livesay in May of 1908.

So where was Phillips before that date? Those who would like to believe that he was indeed Butch Cassidy say it is obvious that he created a new identity for himself after faking his death in South America. However, if the "fake death" did occur in January of 1908, he would not have had time to leave Bolivia, travel to France, undergo plastic surgery, return to the U.S., meet Gertrude and court her, and then marry her all before May 14 of that same year. (Of course, it's possible that Cassidy left South America much earlier and was not involved in the famous January shootout at all.)

Another problem with the claim that Phillips was actually Cassidy is the fact that Phillips was an engineer and mechanic, whereas Cassidy was simply a cowboy — albeit one who was very proficient at robbing banks. When and where would this man have had the opportunity to learn such a trade as engineering? And would he really have been able to make an honest living at it for 25 years?

Phillips's manuscript also had many discrepancies; it was laden with inaccurate facts and wrong dates. It could have been, however, that he had purposely misrepresented events in order to confuse and misinform the authorities.

One more intriguing fact was added to the mix by a man named Evans, who had worked with Phillips from 1921 until 1930, when times had become tough for Phillips's company. Evans recalled that around 1929, a company by the name of Riblet Tramway had offered Phillips a contract to do work for them. Phillips would be overseeing the construction of a new tramway in Bolivia. The contract was a lucrative one, and though the extra money would have been very useful, Phillips had refused the job. Evans thought it strange at the time but later, when he learned that Phillips might actually have been Butch Cassidy, he realized why his colleague might have been reluctant to travel to Bolivia. Perhaps Phillips had suspected that the law down in South America was still looking for him.

Whatever the truth, the people of Spokane came to admire and respect William T. Phillips through the years. He was described as kind, polite, and friendly, and he loved children. A charismatic man, he also enjoyed the company of women and the odd glass of whisky, but could "hold his liquor well." He was also said to be "good with a gun," and the kind of man "who would give you the shirt off his back."

For decades now, the subject of Phillips being Butch Cassidy has been a topic of intense interest for historians. In 1991, it became a segment on the television show *Unsolved Mysteries.* Unfortunately, after the show aired, the mystery became all the more confusing because so many viewers telephoned in afterwards with their own ideas and claims on Cassidy's identity. One caller even claimed to be Cassidy's son, and said his father had passed away in 1978. If that were true, Cassidy would have been 112!

Despite everything, some solid evidence on the Cassidy/Phillips claim does exist. For instance, in the 1970s, a handwriting expert who compared the writing in the last known authentic letter written by Cassidy in 1902 and one written later by Phillips in 1935 concluded that, "the letters were written by the same person," without knowing whose handwriting she was examining. And in 1991, one of the world's most renowned forensic anthropologists visited San Vincente, Bolivia, to exhume bodies in a grave purported to be that of Butch Cassidy and the Sundance Kid. He was only able to locate one skeleton, which appeared to have been the right age and size to match the Sundance Kid, but with the aid of DNA evidence, it turned out to be the remains of a German gentleman named Gustav Zimmer.

Even Cassidy's own family was divided in its opinions as to where and when he died. Most thought he died in the early 1900s in South America. But his youngest sister, Lula Parker Betensen (who wrote a book entitled *Butch Cassidy: My Brother*), claimed her brother had come back to the United States and had visited his family in 1925. The law, she said, "thought he was dead and he was happy to leave it that way. He made us promise not to tell anyone he was alive. It was the tightest family secret. He died peacefully in Spokane in 1937." She did not, however, confirm what name he was using at the time of his death.

If William Thadeus Phillips really was Robert LeRoy Parker (Butch Cassidy), no one gave him away during his 27 years in Spokane, during which time he lived, for the most part, as a respectable citizen. Indeed, if the story is true, then Butch Cassidy's reinvention of himself as William T. Phillips can be considered the finest example in history of a criminal rehabilitating himself back into society.

If, on the other hand, Phillips was not Butch Cassidy, he still managed to contribute to a mystery that the media has perpetuated through the years, one that continues to confound and intrigue all those enquiring minds that want to know the truth.

To this day, the story of Butch Cassidy and William Phillips remains one of the greatest mysteries of the old Wild West. And perhaps that is the way it should stay.

Chapter 8
King of the Bootleggers

rohibition days in the Pacific Northwest certainly allowed for, and even encouraged, rum running and bootlegging, and many people became proficient at the game. Stealing, selling confiscated alcohol, and taking bribes were commonplace, and the men of the Seattle police force — even members of the so-called "Dry Squad" — were by no means exempt from these activities. During the 1920s, one Seattle police officer in particular was able to make a fortune in the bootlegging business, eagerly turning his back on the law to pursue a more profitable lifestyle.

His name was Roy Olmstead, and he was born on

September 18, 1886, on a farm in Beaver City, Nebraska. His parents, John and Sarah, were ordinary farming folk who raised their children to be good citizens. Roy moved to Seattle in 1904, and worked for the Moran Brothers Company shipyard until he was able to join the Seattle Police Department in May of 1907 (where two of his brothers, Frank and Ralph, also served). By 1910, Roy Olmstead had been promoted to sergeant. He rose quickly through the ranks as a result of his natural abilities and instinct for police work.

Then, on November 1, 1914, the citizens of Washington State passed State Initiative Measure Number 3 by a margin of 52 percent. This measure prohibited alcoholic beverages from being manufactured by breweries and distilleries, or from being sold in bars and saloons. It became law on January 12, 1916, and Washington joined the 22 other "dry" states. Despite this, many people in Seattle ignored the new liquor laws. After all, Seattle was a port city, and was usually full of sailors who arrived in town to have a "good time." They and other rowdies soon tarnished Seattle's image.

A year later, on December 11, 1917, Joel "Joe" Warren was appointed Seattle's chief of police, following the resignation of Chief Charles Beckingham. Prior to his appointment, Warren worked as a law enforcement officer throughout Washington State and Alaska, and his impressive record made him the best choice for the challenging position. Warren's orders were to "clean up the town," and he was determined to do just that.

It was not long before Chief Warren's attention was drawn to Sergeant Roy Olmstead. Warren was impressed with Olmstead's enthusiasm and persistence, as well as his squeaky clean record, so he decided to appoint the young man as acting lieutenant, a position that was made permanent on January 22, 1919. Olmstead was the youngest lieutenant on Warren's force at that time and, although he was a large man who struck an imposing figure in uniform, he was soon nicknamed "the baby lieutenant."

Meanwhile, despite the severe prohibition laws, the illegal sale of liquor continued. It seemed there was always someone ready to supply the customer for the right price. In order to put a stop to this, Warren used the Seattle Police Dry Squad to focus on arresting those who were stealing and selling confiscated liquor.

Although Olmstead was not a member of the Dry Squad, he kept a watchful eye on the city's bootleggers and smugglers, studying the small-time operations. He soon realized that many of these petty lawbreakers were getting caught simply because they were not planning their moves more carefully — they were just rushing in, unaware of the police net waiting to catch them.

Olmstead could see that the city's bootleggers and smugglers had no idea how to run a business, and business skills, he knew, were exactly what was needed if a rum running operation was to be successful.

He also knew that there was an enormous amount of good liquor in British Columbia for the taking, and an equally large market for this liquor in Seattle. These two facts spelled profit to Olmstead. Given the correct level of business organization and foresight, bootleggers, he decided, could make a fortune. They just needed to know the right way to go about it. And Olmstead figured he knew the right way.

In the meantime, he still had to carry out his police work. Chief Warren had ordered him to conduct a raid on the LeRoy Hotel, where gambling and drinking were reported to be taking place. Soon after this raid, Warren gave Olmstead orders to arrest several members of the Dry Squad, including the sergeant who had headed up the team. This sergeant, and other Dry Squad members, had been seizing illegal liquor, hiding it, and then reselling it to bootleggers. They were also accused of pocketing some of the money taken from the gambling raids.

Warren was indeed doing everything in his power to clean up the city, and many gamblers, bootleggers, saloon owners, and prostitutes left town because things were getting too hot. For those people, it was no longer exciting to live in a seaport where crime was on the decline and the "good guys" were winning.

Not so, however, for Roy Olmstead, who was continuing to learn a great deal about the bootlegging business. As time passed, Olmstead became convinced that he could outwit the authorities and make money on the side by running a bootlegging operation of his own. He knew how the Dry Squad operated, and was therefore certain that working on the other side of the law would be a piece of cake.

On October 8, 1919, the Volstead, or National Prohibition, Act was passed into law, and things became even stricter. With few exceptions, it was now considered a federal crime to export, sell, manufacture, or transport alcoholic beverages, and a Prohibition Bureau was set up to oversee the enforcement of the law.

By then, Lieutenant Olmstead had already made up his mind to get involved in the bootlegging business. Unfortunately, on one of his first large hoists, prohibition agents had been tipped off about his plans. Early on the morning of March 22, 1920, Olmstead and his "gang of helpers" (who included Seattle Police Sergeant T.J. Clark) were unloading some Canadian whisky from a launch at Meadowdale Dock, three miles north of Edmonds. They were completely unaware that agents had the whole area under surveillance and had barricaded off the only escape route. Though Olmstead managed to avoid capture and bypass the roadblocks by driving his car away through the bushes, he had nonetheless been identified.

Olmstead had eluded the law that day, but soon afterwards he was ordered to surrender to the federal authorities. The Seattle Police Department was informed of his role in the rum running operation, and of his subsequent escape. The whole episode was a great success for the prohibition agents, who had rounded up two police officers, nine bootleggers, six cars, and 100 cases of Canadian whisky. It was the largest seizure in the Puget Sound area to date.

When Olmstead surrendered, he was immediately summoned by Chief Warren to his office. Just three years after having been promoted, the "baby lieutenant" was formally dismissed from the Seattle Police Force. Olmstead was arraigned in court, pleaded guilty as charged, and was fined $500. He took his punishment well, and, realizing he had just learned all the ins and outs of the trade from both sides of the law, he figured he was now free to operate his bootlegging business on a much larger scale. This, of course, was exactly what he had wanted to do in the first place in order to make more money.

Olmstead could now work with larger shipments, bigger and faster vessels, trucks and cars, and additional employees. In fact, before too long, his illegal business had become one of the Puget Sound's biggest employers. Office workers, collectors, bookkeepers, salesmen, drivers, mechanics, rum-running boat crews, warehousemen, and lawyers were all on Olmstead's payroll. He soon owned a fleet of vessels, and purchased a farm outside town to store contraband goods. Within a year, his organization was delivering approximately 200 cases of Canadian liquor to Seattle daily, and Olmstead was making over $200,000 a month — far more than he could have dreamed of making as a policeman. He was now dressing in tailor-made suits, flashing diamond cufflinks, and smoking only the best imported cigars.

Having studied all the tricks of the trade closely, Olmstead understood how to avoid the law and evade the tax being levied by the Canadian government. By buying from distributors and evading Canadian tax, he was able to sell the liquor at least 30 percent cheaper than any of his competitors. This, of course, helped to put many other bootleggers out of business. Olmstead was now the "King."

One thing Roy Olmstead never allowed, however, was for any of his men to carry weapons. Even though rum running was a dangerous business (especially as

Olmstead preferred to undertake hoists in foul weather, when the Coast Guard or hijackers were less likely to be around), he always said he would prefer to lose a shipment of liquor than a man's life. Guns were taboo.

By 1924, Olmstead's racket was known to just about everyone, but he was smart enough now to avoid trouble with the law. He was still a popular figure with many of Seattle's upper crust, including the mayor, local politicians, and important businessmen. They were all aware of his shenanigans but chose to turn a blind eye; after all, many of them were his customers.

That same year, Olmstead divorced his wife, Viola, in order to marry the beautiful Elise Campbell, an Englishwoman from Vancouver, Canada. He then built his new bride an elaborate mansion on Ridgeway Place, overlooking Lake Washington, and they called their house the "snow-white palace."

Soon after their wedding, the Olmsteads founded the American Radio Telephone Company, which they operated from their new home. Alfred Hubbard, a young, up-and-coming inventor who became Olmstead's business partner, built the radio transmitter in one of the bedrooms. The radio station became known as Station KFOX (later KOMO), and was Seattle's first commercial broadcasting station. Using the name "Aunt Vivian," Elise Olmstead broadcast children's

Olmstead and his wife, photographed in 1925

bedtime stories over the airwaves, but prohibition agents immediately suspected these stories were actually coded messages for Olmstead's run-running vessels.

Though authorities knew a great deal about

Olmstead's bootlegging operation, it was virtually impossible to catch him "in the act." There were so many islands in the Pacific Northwest where smugglers could hide, and so much water for the federal agents to constantly patrol, that it was easy for smugglers to slip through the net of prohibition enforcement.

So, Roy Olmstead was able to carry on with his business. But two men from the Federal Prohibition Bureau continued to work hard behind the scenes to bring him down. These men were Roy C. Lyle, the administrator for Washington State, and his chief assistant, William Whitney, and both were determined to prosecute Olmstead for violation of federal prohibition laws.

Then, in September of 1924, Alfred Hubbard decided to inform on Olmstead in exchange for a job with the prohibition agents. Lyle and Whitney were delighted to have an "informant" inside the Olmstead organization; they knew that Hubbard was extremely conversant with all aspects of Olmstead's operations.

One month later, Canadian Customs officials seized the *Eva B*, which was owned by Olmstead, and confiscated over 700 cases of liquor. They arrested the men onboard, who promptly squealed on Olmstead and his gang. At the same time, the Prohibition Bureau also set up wiretaps on numerous telephones throughout the city, including ones at Olmstead's house, and quickly became privy to all the discussions taking place.

Whitney knew that with the information he'd gathered from informants, plus the wiretapping conversations, he had more than enough evidence to warrant a raid on the Olmsteads' "palace." So, on November 17, 1924, he and his men entered the mansion while Olmstead and his wife were entertaining 16 guests, and confiscated numerous cases of bootlegged liquor. Olmstead's attorney, Jerry Finch, also had his office raided, where incriminating records of Olmstead's business were found and confiscated; Whitney was now convinced that he had enough evidence for a grand jury investigation.

As the investigation got underway, Olmstead continued business as usual, apparently unperturbed. However, at 2 a.m. on Thanksgiving morning, November 26, federal agents made more arrests. Nine people, five automobiles (including the King County sheriff's squad car), a rum-running launch known as *Three Deuces*, and 240 cases of contraband liquor were all seized. Both Roy and Elise Olmstead were among the nine arrested, and on January 19, 1925, a two-count indictment against Roy Olmstead was returned by the Federal Grand Jury.

The trial that began that month proved to be one of the largest and most controversial in American history.

The Federal Grand Jury had indicted Roy Olmstead and 89 defendants for violation of the National Prohibition Act. Some of the defendants escaped to Canada before the trial. Others put in guilty pleas, and some were simply dismissed for lack of evidence. Eventually, the number of defendants dropped to 29.

Olmstead's lawyers maintained that the wiretapping was illegal and should not be allowed as evidence. However, when Olmstead's trial ended on February 20, 1926, 21 of the 29 defendants were convicted, including Roy Olmstead and his attorney, Jerry Finch. Elise and seven other defendants were acquitted. Olmstead was fined $8000 and sentenced to four years in the McNeil Island Federal Penitentiary. Finch was fined $500 and sentenced to two years. Other sentences ranged from 15 months to three years.

During Olmstead's incarceration at McNeil Island, he made frequent appeals to higher courts. His main argument always centered on the fact that wiretapping was illegal and unconstitutional. In his opinion, and in the opinion of many others, wiretapping contravened a person's right to privacy under the Fourth and Fifth Amendments.

In February of 1928, the U.S. Supreme Court heard the famous *Olmstead v. the United States* case, in which Olmstead argued that wiretaps constituted an "unrea-

sonable search and seizure" within the meaning of the
Fourth Amendment. He also claimed that the "evidence" obtained compelled the defendants "to be witnesses against themselves," which was in violation of
the Fifth Amendment.

Olmstead had indeed studied the law well.
Nonetheless, while the Court did not totally dispute that
"the mode of obtaining [the evidence] was unethical
and a misdemeanor under the law of Washington," it
maintained that anyone who installs in his house a telephone with connecting wires intends to "project his
voice to those quite outside, and that the wires beyond
his house and messages while passing over them" are
not protected by the Fourth Amendment.

It was a clever ploy, but wiretapping was still considered a "dirty business" by many at the trial, including
Justice Oliver Wendell Holmes. He stated that the courts
were "apt to err by sticking too closely to the words of
a law."

However, the government's right to use wiretapping had been affirmed, and Olmstead lost his appeal.
He was returned to McNeil Island Penitentiary in the
custody of U.S. Marshals on June 28, 1928, to complete
his four-year sentence.

On May 12, 1931, Olmstead was released from
prison. Elise met him at the dock in Steilacoom, and

together they drove back to Seattle to begin a new life. By that time, the days of bootlegging were drawing to a close. After various amendments to repeal prohibition and the Volstead Act, the Prohibition Amendment Act was finally introduced into Congress in February of 1933, and was ratified by 36 states in December of that year.

On Christmas Day of 1935, due to Elise Olmstead's relentless petitioning on behalf of her husband, President Franklin D. Roosevelt granted Roy Olmstead a full pardon. All of Olmstead's constitutional rights — along with his initial $8000 fine and another $2288 in court fees — were restored to him.

But something had happened to Roy Olmstead during his years in prison. He was no longer the same man. To begin with, he had converted to the Christian Science faith and now believed that liquor was a curse to society. Following his release from prison, he decided to make his living as a furniture salesman. He then opened a Christian Science office in town, and also became a Sunday school teacher and conducted Bible study courses. Roy Olmstead was a changed man.

Obviously, Elise Olmstead did not particularly like the man her husband had become because on May 28, 1943, she filed for divorce, claiming he had "deserted her without just cause." The divorce was made final on

August 5 of that year, and nothing more was heard of the enterprising Elise.

Roy Olmstead continued to lead the life of an upright citizen. Up until the time of his death, he remained an active member of the community, helping others who had fallen by the wayside. He never missed a Monday morning visit to the King County jail to talk with prisoners on the evils of drink. Many alcoholics were released into his custody from jail for him to counsel and help rehabilitate. The "good cop" had returned.

Olmstead gave his last interview to the press shortly before his death in 1966. He was asked at that time why he had never carried a gun on his rum-running expeditions, and why he had never allowed his men to carry guns, as so many other bootleggers were always armed. The old Roy Olmstead returned for a moment as he replied with a grin, "I figured if old Roy couldn't talk his way out of trouble it was a lost cause."

Roy Olmstead, King of the Bootleggers, died on April 30, 1966, at the age of 80, having spent the last 35 years of his life living on the right side of the law, and attempting to convert others to do the same. Despite this, he will always be best remembered for his earlier escapades as a bootlegger extraordinaire in the rum-running era.

Chapter 9
The Man Who Loved Sinners

**any** honorable men tried to rid Washington State of crime during the early years of the 20th century. Some were relentless in their pursuit of criminals, and many were successful in catching them. None, however, was more colorful than the Reverend Dr. Mark Matthews, an early Washington State preacher. His aim was to convert the area's criminals, setting them on the path of righteousness, and he delivered his message with fire and brimstone for over four decades.

Reverend Matthews was the epitome of the Wild West preacher. A Southerner by birth, he was ordained at the age of 20 and arrived in the Pacific Northwest in

1902, at the age of 35, to take up the position of minister at Seattle's First Presbyterian Church. Standing well over six feet tall, Matthews struck an imposing figure as he walked through town dressed in his long black coat and black hat, as well as the high stiff collar and string tie favored by most clerics at the time. With his pale complexion, thin nose, and long, curly locks, some thought he looked a trifle effeminate. But no one dared say this to his face — his loud, passionate preaching put the fear of God into sinners and non-sinners alike.

The reverend's preaching was targeted primarily at those he considered to be "the bad guys." These were the bootleggers, the gamblers, the prostitutes, the corrupt officials, and the communists. It was said that before he accepted the position at the First Presbyterian Church, he had come to Seattle to look around. When he'd noticed a gambling establishment in the community, he'd announced loudly for all to hear, "Either that must go, or I will not stay here!" Though the gambling hall did not go, Matthews, after much persuasion, agreed to stay, and for the next 40 years his confrontations with gambling establishments and liquor vendors in the city were cause for a great deal of fiery rhetoric.

His strong beliefs and passionate sermons brought scores of new members into the Church. Under his guidance, the congregation grew from 1000 parishioners in 1903 to 8000 by 1940. In fact, Matthews' church became the largest Presbyterian Church in the country. In 1907, it was given a new home at Seventh and Spring Streets and, as the years passed, 28 Sunday schools and missions throughout the city were needed to accommodate the ever-growing congregation. Broadcasting his sermons via Station KTW (the first church-owned radio station in the United States) also helped to increase the reverend's listening audience.

Matthews was a well-known fundamentalist, and played a significant role in the fundamentalist–modernist conflict within the northern Presbyterian Church. He was the moderator at the General Assembly in 1913, after which he strongly urged the Church to go back to the "fundamentals."

Matthews' strict, no-nonsense message also brought him many enemies. By 1914, in company with other church leaders, he had entered into a fierce battle to destroy the saloons throughout the state. If there was ever a shady establishment that Matthews hated above all the others, it was the saloon. In one of his heated sermons, the reverend insisted to his congregation that the saloon was "the most fiendish, corrupt, and hell-soaked institution that ever crawled out of the slime of the eternal pit." In another sermon, he explained that a saloon "takes your sweet, innocent daughter, robs her of virtue, and transforms her into a brazen, wanton harlot." His very presence overwhelmed and dominated crowds as he called for "the death of sin," and his lectures played an important role in the eventual passing of Initiative Number 3, the statewide prohibition law.

Matthews was also full of contradictions. He manipulated his congregation when necessary by informing them of available jobs and challenging others to offer competitive salaries. He was openly opposed to the women's suffrage movement and firmly against the movement to ordain women as elders in the Presbyterian Church. He was a compelling, even idiosyncratic character.

It did not, however, bother Reverend Matthews one iota that many of his views were unpopular because an equal number of his works for humane causes earned him high praise. He organized an open-air camp for those with tuberculosis, opened up a kindergarten, established Seattle's first daycare nursery, and helped create the city's first juvenile court. In addition, he was president of the King County Red Cross and the local Humane Society, and the driving force behind an Italian earthquake relief fund in 1909.

Despite these many accomplishments, Matthews was still known best for his relentless pursuit and rehabilitation of bootleggers and other criminals. After seeing to it that these lawbreakers were arrested, he would then do his best to convert them to a straight and narrow path. He hated the sins but loved the sinners, who became fodder for his religious beliefs.

Not long after his appointment to Seattle's First Presbyterian Church, Matthews was granted an honorary Seattle Police Department badge and a special duty sheriff's badge, which he carried with him for years. During those years, however, he only made use of the police badge's power to make one arrest. The man he arrested was none other than the chief of police himself, Charles Wappenstein — the very same man who had issued the badge to Matthews in the first place.

Wappenstein had been suspected of protecting and financing a Seattle prostitution ring, and Reverend Matthews would not rest until he had revealed this corruption. Using money secretly borrowed from his insurance companies, Matthews hired an investigator from the Burns Detective Agency to investigate Wappenstein and other influential citizens, including Mayor Hiram Gill, whom Matthews also considered to be "not pure." When he found out that his suspicions were correct, he arrested Wappenstein and spearheaded a recall of Mayor Gill. Meanwhile, he fought just as vigorously from his pulpit for other men whose characters were being unfairly blackened by the scandal.

The Man Who Loved Sinners

In 1916, still hell bent on bringing down crooked-ness in high places, the fiery pastor financed a phony gambling ring to uncover more police corruption. Eight years later, in a 1924 poll, Matthews was listed among the top 25 most influential Protestant ministers in the nation. His words were always powerful, and his ser-mons held strong and frightening messages — even if listeners did not always share his beliefs, his very pres-ence and demeanor had the potential to make them think twice.

In 1940, the Reverend Dr. Mark Matthews passed away at the age of 73. His funeral was attended by many of Washington's best. The governor, mayors, and many public officials were among the mourners, and every florist shop within Seattle's city limits was sold out of flowers by the end of the day. Police were called in to control the throng of people who lined the streets out-side the church. Everyone, it seemed, wanted to pay their last respects to a man who had made such an impact on society.

Throughout his four decades in Seattle, the fiery preacher had collected millions of dollars for national and foreign missions. After his death, it was discovered that his own bank account only contained a few dollars.

In addition to being a compelling force in Seattle's early history, and a strong religious and political figure in his day, the Reverend Mark Matthews was one of the most egotistical and extraordinary Christian leaders in the west. He had chosen to bring his ministry to a city where the majority of the population was far from pious or church-going, and through the sheer force of his personality he was able to increase his congregation to astonishing numbers. Though he was a man of the cloth who abhorred the evils of sin and violence, he was reported to have kept a pair of pearl-handled pistols in his office desk, earning him the title of the "pistol-packing parson."

Matthews was loved, hated, and even feared by many people, but by the end of his life, he had gained the respect of everyone. He changed the moral face of Seattle and played a large part in helping to rid Washington State of the criminal element that was rampant in those early years.

Throughout his life, and even after his demise, Matthews had also constantly attracted the attention of the Seattle press. They found him fascinating and enigmatic — a man who was on a continual religious rampage against everything from bootlegging and police corruption to the simple pleasure of playing a game of bridge.

Of course, had the reverend totally succeeded in his quest for righteousness, there would have been no tales to tell of the past indiscretions and nefarious crimes from Washington State's outlawed history.

Epilogue

On November 11, 1889, Washington became the 42nd state in the Union. That day, President Benjamin Harrison and Secretary of State James Blaine both signed the proclamation with a pen made of gold that had been mined in Washington Territory. It was an auspicious beginning.

Despite this momentous occasion, which gave respectability and credence to a somewhat wild territory, there were many remnants of rowdy behavior still existing within the newly formed state. Indeed, Washington State would be in for some unruly times ahead.

When thinking of the Wild West and the villains and outlaws who made up those exciting times in America's history, most of us do not think of Washington State. Instead, we think of California, Wyoming, Utah, Colorado, or Texas, where outlaws roamed and ruled, breaking laws and wreaking havoc. Washington State, however, also abounded with villains and outlaws whose stories were just as fascinating and whose crimes just as perverse and corrupt as those committed by scoundrels in other states.

Epilogue

All the preceding stories were about real men and women in Washington State's past, most of whom became legends in their own lifetimes. They lived in an era when smuggling was rife, liquor was plentiful (despite prohibition), murder was rampant, and human life was not held in much regard. And while most of them were feared, hunted, or even despised in their day, perhaps now they will also all be remembered as colorful characters who were merely products of the times in which they lived.

Certainly all their names will live on in the annals of criminal history.

Acknowledgments

For help with my research into Washington State's criminal history and the scoundrels who lived there over 100 years ago, I am indebted to many people. I would especially like to thank David Hastings of the Office of The Secretary of State, Archives Division, Olympia; Nancy Compau of the Spokane Library; the staff at The Museum of History & Industry in Seattle; the Tacoma Sheriff's Office; Jim Dullenty for supplying me with a rare copy of *The Bandit Invincible*; Juanita Todd for allowing me to tell Esther Sundquist Bower's unusual story; and Terese Cateriano for supplying photographic material of "Byrd's boxes." Other photographic material comes courtesy of the Museum of History & Industry in Seattle, and the Division of Archives & Records Management in Olympia.

The Author acknowledges the following sources for quotes used in this book: *Washington — The First Hundred Years (1889-1989)*, by Don Duncan; *The Reverend Mark Matthews: An Activist in the Progressive Era*, by Dale E. Soden; *The Seattle Daily Times;* Inventory of the William T. Phillips Manuscript Collection, Utah State Historical Society; Correspondence &

Acknowledgments

Commitment Records, courtesy of Secretary of State (Archives and Records); *The Hunting of Harry Tracy*, a Gaslight e-text; and the History Link Database, Seattle/King County.

My thanks to Jill Foran for an excellent, meticulous editing job.

And lastly, I would like to thank my own family for allowing me the time and space to explore another world far removed from my own.

Photo credits

Cover: Washington State Archives; **Seattle Post — Intelligencer Collection, Museum of History and Industry:** pg 107; **Washington State Archives:** pgs 16, 27, 31, 58, 75, 83.

Bibliography

Carpenter, Cecelia. *Leschi: Last Chief of the Nisquallies.* Heritage Quest, 1986.

Clark, Cecil. *B.C. Provincial Police Stories.* Surrey, BC: Heritage House Publishing Co., 1989.

Clark, Norman C. *Washington: A Bicentennial History.* New York: W.W. Norton & Company Inc., 1976.

Dryden, Cecil. *Dryden's History of Washington.* Portland: Binfords & Mort Publishers, 1968.

Duncan, Don. *Washington — The First One Hundred Years, 1889-1989.* Seattle Times Company, 1989.

Dullenty, Jim. Various articles from 1975 to 1986 in *Old West Magazine, True West Magazine* and *Quarterly of the National Association of Outlaw and Lawmen History* (NOLA).

Horan, James D. *The Great American West.* New York: Crown Publishers Inc., 1994.

Bibliography

Meadows, Anne. *Digging Up Butch & Sundance.* New York: St. Martin's Press, 1994.

Meeker, Ezra. *Tragedy of Leschi.* Seattle: Museum of History & Industry, 1980.

Meeker, Ezra. *Pioneer Reminiscences of Puget Sound.* Seattle, Museum of History & Industry, 1980.

O'Neill, Bill. *Encyclopedia of Western Gunfighters.* University of Oklahoma Press, 1991.

Phillips, William T. *The Bandit Invincible.* Montana: Rocky Mountain House Press, 1986.

Pointer, Larry. *In Search of Butch Cassidy.* Norman, Oklahoma: University of Oklahoma Press, 1977.

Sale, Roger. *Seattle, Past to Present.* Seattle: University of Washington Press, 1976.

Soden, Dale E. *The Reverend Mark Matthews: An Activist in the Progressive Era.* Seattle: University of Washington Press, 2000.

About the Author

Valerie Green was born and educated in England but has lived in Victoria, British Columbia, since 1968, where she pursues a career as a freelance writer, columnist for a local newspaper, and author of many historical books set in the Pacific Northwest, including family biographies.